Write with WORLD II

Learning to Create an Informed Opinion, Respond to Controversy, and Persuade Effectively

Student Edition

Dr. Ronald L. Pitcock
Dr. Jennifer Workman Pitcock
Dr. Rayshelle Dietrich
Contributors from *God's World News* and *WORLD Magazine*

God's World Publications, Inc.
Asheville, NC

Published by God's World Publications, Inc.

Printed in the United States of America.

ISBN: 978-0-9855957-3-9

About the authors:

Ron Pitcock, General Editor and Author, is the J. Vaughn and Evelyn H. Wilson Honors Fellow at Texas Christian University in Fort Worth, Texas. He earned his Ph.D. in English and American Literature at the University of Kentucky.

A National Writing Project Fellow, Dr. Pitcock was recently named one of the top 300 professors in the United States by The Princeton Review. Dr. Pitcock has also received the "Promising Researcher Award" from the National Council of Teachers of English and the 2010 Wassenich Award for Mentoring in the TCU Community. His approach to teaching writing has led to multiple teaching awards at the University of Kentucky, Indiana State University, and TCU, where he was named TCU's "Honors Professor of the Year" and chosen by students as the recipient of the 2009 TCU Inspirational Professor Award presented by EECU.

Each summer, Dr. Pitcock spends a month in Europe eating gelato (and teaching Honors students a little too). When he's not traveling the world, he enjoys spending time at the swimming pool with his wife and three children.

Jenny Pitcock, Associate Editor and Author, has served as a writer for *God's World News* since 2005 and currently serves as a news writer and editor. She earned her Ph.D. in American Literature at the University of Kentucky. She is a Fellow of the National Writing Project and has received teaching awards at the University of Kentucky, most notably the Chancellor's Award for Most Outstanding Teaching Assistant in the University.

A mother of three living in Fort Worth Texas, Dr. Pitcock is an avid reader and freelance writer. She loves nothing more than spending time with her family—though she occasionally sneaks away to Starbucks to relax and read a good book.

Rayshelle Dietrich, Author, lives in Fort Worth with her husband and three energetic children. She earned her Ph.D. in American Literature from Texas Christian University where she was awarded the College of Liberal Arts Graduate Teacher of the Year. When she isn't reading Dr. Seuss with her kids or sneaking veggies into their food, she enjoys doing archival work to recover the diaries and letters of local women.

Contributors from *God's World News* and *WORLD Magazine*:

Krieg Barrie, Illustrator, *WORLD Magazine*
Emily Belz, Reporter, *WORLD Magazine*
Joel Belz, Founder, *God's World News* and *WORLD Magazine*
Mindy Belz, Editor, *WORLD Magazine*
Rich Bishop, Creative Director, *God's World News*
Anthony Bradley, Correspondent, *WORLD Magazine*
Howard Brinkman, Publisher, *God's World News*
Janie B. Cheaney, Senior Writer, *WORLD Magazine*
Rebecca Cochrane, Editor, *God's World News*
Jamie Dean, News Editor, *WORLD Magazine*
Victoria Drake, Editor, *God's World News*
Megan Dunham, Writer, *God's World News*
Amy Henry, Correspondent, *WORLD Magazine*
Roy McGinnis, Writer, *God's World News*
Mickey McLean, Web Executive Editor, worldmag.com
Marvin Olasky, Editor-in-Chief, *World News Group*
Susan Olasky, Senior Writer, *WORLD Magazine*
Arsenio Orteza, Correspondent, *WORLD Magazine*
Edward Lee Pitts, Reporter, *WORLD Magazine*
Patti Richter, Writer, *God's World News*
Warren Smith, Vice President, *World News Group*
Kim Stegall, Editor, *God's World News*
James Allen Walker, Photojournalist, *WORLD Magazine*

CONTENTS

Write with WORLD

WRITING CURRICULUM

GENERAL INTRODUCTION

DON'T SKIP THIS PART!

Some jet around the world, writing history as they watch it take place. Others work from home, creating imaginary worlds in words—worlds where children wish they could live. Some follow clues and discover stories that would have been lost to history without their research.

Adventurer, artist, and detective—these are all roles writers play. If you ask most writers, they'll tell you they love what they do. It's different every day. Often, they get to interview interesting people. They visit fascinating places. They're always learning new things. And they have something to say.

We believe you have something to say too. In *Write with WORLD*, we want to help you learn how. We think the best way to learn writing is from people who are actually doing it.

THE REAL DEAL

In this writing program, real, professional writers will be sharing what they have to say with you. In each lesson, a writer from *WORLD Magazine* or *God's World News* will share tips on how they read, think, or write.

As the year progresses, these writers may even read some of your writing. A few of you will even have your writing published online or in one of the magazines.

CALLING ALL WRITERS

From the very first lesson, we're going to treat you like real writers. You may be thinking, "Wait! I've tried writing before and I'm just no good at it." We suspect that's not the problem.

You see, we've looked at a lot of writing programs for students. Most were filled with what we'd call "canned" writing assignments. They ask students to do things like describe the family car or tell how to make a peanut butter and jelly sandwich.

We don't blame you if you're not good at this type of writing. It's an exercise. It doesn't really ask you to think. Many of you probably find it boring.

Real writers get interesting assignments with purpose. They write with the expectation that their writing will be published. We're going to do our best to create assignments that interest you and opportunities for others to see what you have to say.

FINDING YOUR VOICE

If you have a favorite writer, you may be able to recognize his writing even before you see his name on the cover. He may have certain words he likes to use. Or a distinct sense of humor that carries over from book to book. Or a way of putting sentences together that just *sounds* like him. These things together make up a writer's "voice."

If you haven't found your voice yet, *Write with WORLD* can help. We're going to show you how to better "listen" to others' writing. We'll demonstrate and practice how to use words well. And in the process, we believe you'll realize you have ideas worth writing about—and that you're much better at it than you ever imagined.

WHY WRITE?

We believe that Christians should be the best writers. In a world where so many people think there are many truths, Christians know better. The Bible tells us God is the God of truth (Psalm 31:5). God has given us the truth in his Word. Therefore, our writing should not rest on opinions or fads. It should stand the test of logic and time.

Writing is a gift from God. In fact, it's the means through which God chose to preserve his own Word through the ages. And he's still using Christian journalists, novelists, and songwriters to reach the world today.

Who knows what God has planned for you? Maybe someday you'll write a novel that God will use to draw people to him. Or maybe you'll write for your own enjoyment, keeping a journal or blog about your family. Whatever the case, we hope *Write with WORLD* will inspire you to write to the glory of God.

Write with
WORLD

WHAT WRITERS WILL NEED FOR THIS LESSON:
▶ Your writer's journal
▶ Dictionary
▶ Thesaurus
▶ Paper

CAPSULE 1   1.1.1

WHAT IS JOURNALISM?

If you completed *Write with WORLD I*, most of the writing you did was about yourself. You gathered most of your information by examining your personal experiences. In *Write with WORLD II*, we'll begin looking outward. In this unit we will learn a specific type of writing called journalism. Journalism is gathering and reporting the news, either in written (for newspapers and the Internet) or spoken (for television and radio) form.

Journalism's writing style is geared toward getting information across quickly and **succinctly**. News stories are written with busy readers in mind. Each story's headline is designed to grab attention. A good headline should also let readers know enough about the story to determine whether or not they want to read it. In the story itself, the key information comes right at the beginning. Readers should know what the story is about after reading the lead (first paragraph). The lead is a short paragraph that summarizes the story. The following paragraphs add details. Readers should be able to get an idea of the day's news by skimming headlines and leads.

In most cases, regular news stories focus on current events—activities that have happened or will happen soon. These events are of interest to the community that reads that particular newspaper. For instance, if you live in a small town in Georgia, your town's peach festival might be front page news. It's a big event in your community. However, that story probably won't get printed in any other newspapers—it's not relevant to most readers outside of Smalltown, Georgia.

The people who gather the news and write news stories are called journalists or reporters. Good reporters should be **objective**. They convey facts and provide perspective to communicate clearly and efficiently. Reporters write precisely; they don't include **jargon**. Whenever possible, they use straightforward, simple sentence constructions. They write in active voice and use strong verbs whenever possible. This simple, active style helps keep stories concise.

A news story shouldn't be any longer than necessary. It should include facts, beginning with the most important information and moving to the least important. Paragraphs are short—sometimes just a sentence or two. The point of the news is to communicate information. Adding in extra words and flowery phrasing can stand in the way of getting the message across. A good rule to keep in mind is "never use a big word when a smaller one will do."

This type of writing may sound much different than what you did in *Write with WORLD I*. However, there are similarities in all good writing. Just like a narrative, a news story must be organized. Often, news stories tell about an event, so you will use chronological order. In both narratives and news stories, strong verbs keep the writing lively and hold readers' interest. And all good writing requires accurate description. Whether you're writing about the time you were lost at sea or describing the homecoming parade for your community paper, your ability to create a picture in the reader's mind using words is the key to successful communication.

STYLE TIME

 Today we talked a little about journalistic style. You want your writing to be as easy to understand as possible. That means not using lots of big words or long sentences. What we do write should be correct, though.

Through our years of teaching, one typical problem we've seen is comma splices. It's a form of run-on sentence. While a fused sentence is two independent clauses smashed together with no punctuation, a comma splice hooks two independent clauses together but sticks a comma between them:

I rode the bus to school, I walked home.

There are four ways to fix this problem:
1. Make it into two sentences.
I rode the bus to school. I walked home.

2. Add a coordinating conjunction after the comma.
*I rode the bus to school, **but** I walked home.*

3. Make one of your two independent clauses into a dependent clause by adding a subordinating conjunction.
***After** I rode the bus to school, I walked home.*

4. If the sentences are closely related ideas, you may link them using a semicolon.
I rode the bus to school; I walked home.

How you choose to fix the problem will depend on a couple of things. The first is the meaning of your sentence. "I rode the bus to school, but I walked home," doesn't mean exactly the same thing as "After I rode the bus to school, I walked home." You want to make sure your fix doesn't give the sentence a different meaning.

Another is the style of the piece you're writing. For instance, in journalistic style, you want simple sentences. In most cases, you would do fix number 1—divide the comma splice into two different simple sentences.

That's it for today! After you finish your article in capsule 1.1.5, you'll practice looking for comma splices and fixing them.

CAPSULE 2   1.1.2

FINDING THE NEWS

In this unit, we want you to become reporters. We don't want you to simply learn to write a news story—that's only part of what a reporter does. A real reporter is always looking for a story. To be good at your job, you need to know what's going on in your corner of the world. Then you need to think about what events are news—current events that are of interest to your community.

Being a reporter has lots of similarities to being a detective. If you've ever seen a crime show on television, you'll remember that police detectives and news reporters get to the scene of the crime as quickly as possible. Both want to learn as many details of the crime as they can—the police detective so that he can solve the crime, and the reporter so that he can report exactly what happened. Both will try to talk to witnesses. Both will look for any clues left at the scene. When they've gathered all the information they can, both will create a timeline and try to figure out how all the facts that they have fit together to create a narrative (story) of the event.

For now, your first job as a reporter is to begin looking for possible stories. If you're going to a basketball tournament this upcoming weekend, think like a reporter. As you watch each game, note important plays. Who scored the winning basket? Was anyone injured? Did a player foul out? Which game would make the best story?

As you begin watching for good stories, start reading the news. The best way to learn a particular style of writing is to read as much of it as possible. If you receive *Top Story* or *Trak*, sit down with a copy and read through it. Or if your family receives a daily newspaper, examine the stories. In which paragraph do you discover what the story is about? How long are most sentences? Most paragraphs? The more you read, the better you will write.

WORLD WISDOM

WORLD *Magazine* reporter Emily Belz gives advice on how to find topics for news stories:

First, listen to what smart and interesting people around you—friends, family—are talking about. We try to tell each other the most interesting things in our lives, so regular old conversations are rich soil for story ideas (unless everyone you know only talks about science fiction or Olympic curling or something).

When I first moved to Washington, D.C., I heard stories from some of my friends about how the tour guides in the Capitol told a lot of whoppers to their tour groups. So I went and followed a bunch of tours around and found out the amateur tour guides were indeed telling tall tales. I heard one tour guide tell her group that Pocahontas married John Smith, which isn't true—though they do fall in love in the Disney movie. Don't worry: Today only professional guides who know what they're talking about are supposed to give tours in the Capitol.

Second, follow your curiosity, and keep following it. In 2010, I heard Secretary of State Hillary Clinton give a speech at the National Prayer Breakfast where she spent about five minutes talking about a great adoption home she and Mother Teresa opened in Washington, D.C., in the 1990s. A simple question popped into my head: I wonder how that adoption home is doing now? So after the speech, I called the home—and the line was disconnected. Hm. I looked at a map of where the home was, and saw there was a church next door, so I called them to see if they knew what happened to the home. The pastor told me that the home had shut down years ago. Then she told me where I could get in touch with some of the nuns who worked with the adoption home. The nuns said they had sold the house eight years ago. There you have a story, just from a teaspoon of curiosity!

CWJ

IN YOUR JOURNAL ▶

For this lesson, we don't want you to investigate a crime—that's a difficult task even for an experienced reporter! If you completed *Write with WORLD I*, look at 3.1.3 in your journal.

If not, on a scrap sheet of paper, write the days of the week across the top, like this:

Sunday   Monday   Tuesday   Wednesday   Thursday   Friday   Saturday

Next, under each day list the scheduled activities you have on that day—schooling, music lessons, sports, clubs, church worship and activities, volunteer work, and so on.

After making this chart, think about the activities and interests that fill up your days. Can you add anything that you do occasionally, but not every week, like babysitting for a neighbor or going to the movies with friends? Don't forget activities that are seasonal—like swimming in the pool during the summer or performing in a drama last spring.

Many of these activities involve a community—a group of people who share the same interest and enjoy the same activity. A community doesn't have to be a large group—just a few people who share an interest can be a community.

Which activities that you participate in have communities? List them in your CWJ. Now choose one and make a little chart, like this:

Soccer

Activities/Events   *Issues*

Write down things that might be of interest to your community. In soccer, on the "activities/events" side, you might list games, fundraising events, tournaments, injuries to players, and so on. These can be events that have already occurred (like a recent championship game), or events that are upcoming (such as a team fundraiser.) Be as specific as possible. On the "issues" side, write down topics that have to do with soccer but may not deal directly with you or your team. These should be issues that people disagree on, like how old kids should be when they begin playing select or elite soccer, or whether using your head to hit the ball makes soccer too dangerous to play.

Next, make a list like this one for each community you are part of—a minimum of five total. This may seem like a lot, but once you get going, you'll probably find you have many more. Church, school or homeschool, youth group, sports teams, music groups, neighborhood—these are just a few examples of communities where you are a member. You're also part of the community where you live—your home-town. Almost every town, no matter how small, has some sort of agricultural festival, fair, or parade.

When you've made lists for at least five communities, look back through each. Circle at least two or three "activities/events" or "issues" you think might make interesting news stories.

CAPSULE 3 1.1.3

WHAT SHOULD I INCLUDE?

Did you read through some news stories as we recommended in the last capsule? If so, did you notice how most stories are organized? Organizing a news story is often illustrated as an inverted pyramid or triangle:

At the widest part—the top of your upside down triangle—you include the most important information. The first paragraph (or two at most), should answer the 5W's: "Who? What? Where? When? Why?" It should also answer "How?" if needed.

Next, you should include the most important details. As you get down toward the triangle's tip, you can include other background information that could be helpful to readers. As we've already said, this organization allows readers to get the most **salient** points of the story by reading the headline and the first paragraph or two.

This inverted pyramid organization is useful for newspaper editors as well. Many of the stories printed in local newspapers are shared by news organizations. For instance *God's World News* is a member of the Associated Press (AP). That means we may use AP stories in our papers. The inverted pyramid structure allows an editor to quickly edit a story without having to do a full rewrite. He can cut the story anywhere after the first paragraph or two without worrying that he's cutting key information.

So how would this "inverted pyramid" look if you were writing an actual news story? Let's say you are writing a news story about a basketball team that won the district championship game by making a three-pointer right at the buzzer. As you get ready to write, make sure you have answers for all of your questions:

Who—The Greencastle Fighting Eagles
What—won the district championship
When—last night
Where—at the Putnam High School gym
Why—(not necessary in this story)
How—Hank Pittman scored a three-pointer to break the score, which was tied 76-76.

You would then write a lead (sometimes called a lede) that included all your key information:

> *"In the Putnam County High gym last night, crowds held their breath as Hank Pittman lobbed a shot toward the Greencastle Fighting Eagle's basket right before the final buzzer. The ball rolled around the rim twice before swooshing through, breaking a 76-76 tie and winning another district championship for the Fighting Eagles."*

After reading your lead, readers would know the most important facts of the game: the Fighting Eagles won the district championship with a last-second tie-breaking shot made by Hank Pittman.

In subsequent paragraphs, you would include other important details of the game. You might take readers through the key moments of the game chronologically. You would want to include details such as high scorers for each team, individual and team fouls, and other important statistics. You would also want to tell readers what the next move for the team will be. Do they move on to regionals? Where will regionals take place?

As you narrow down to the end of your story, you might include background information like the team's record so far this season, whether they've won the district championship in the past, and so on.

CWJ

In this lesson, we will be writing a short news story on an event that has taken place or will take place in one of your communities. Look back at your CWJ for 1.1.2. Which activities or events did you circle? Is there one that interests you in particular?

Once you've chosen an event, consider what kind of story it would make. Can you picture the event in your mind? Are there plenty of details that you could describe? Is there background information that you could include? Your ability to create an interesting story will depend partly on the activity you choose. Describing a recent field hockey game will probably make a more exciting story than a meeting of the local gardening club.

In your CWJ today, answer the "5 W's and How" about the event you plan to write about in your news story. Use the example of the district championship as a model. Once you have answered the questions, write a lead for your story.

When writing your lead, keep in mind that your first sentence will either "hook" readers or bore them. So you want to try to grab attention. If you were writing a story about skydivers in an airshow, "There was an air show in Normal, Illinois," is a boring lead. "Yesterday, five men dropped out of an airplane over Normal, Illinois," will get readers' attention.

NOTE: If you can't answer the 5 W's about your story, you should go back to your list and choose another event.

CAPSULE 4   1.1.4

READING THE NEWS

In the previous capsule, we learned about the structure of a news story—the inverted pyramid. Unless you were previously aware of this structure, you probably haven't noticed it as you've read news stories.

Today, we're going to read a news story, looking for the pyramid organization as well as other elements of journalistic style. By "tuning in" to journalistic style, you can improve your own writing. As you read examples, pay attention to how writers use the pyramid organization. As you read each paragraph, note mentally (or in the margins) what kind of information each paragraph contains.

Take a look at this story from the September 2011 issue of *News Current*:

Unearthing Gath

Archeologists are digging up clues about the ancient city of Gath, where yearly excavations have taken place since 1996. This year's dig adds to the wealth of objects already uncovered. One hundred diggers from Canada, South Korea, the United States, and elsewhere began work last week.

In one square hole, several Philistine jugs nearly 3000 years old were being unearthed. Painted decorations often used in Greek art were found on a pottery shard, pointing to the Philistines' origins in the Aegean.

The Philistines, who lived between Gath and Israel, were dreaded enemies of the Israelites.

Gath's most famous bad guy was the giant warrior Goliath. I Samuel 17 tells the familiar Bible story of how Goliath was killed by the shepherd boy David. Diggers have discovered pottery shards containing names similar to Goliath.

Paragraph 1 answers the 5 W's:

Who—One hundred diggers from Canada, South Korea, the United States and elsewhere
What—are digging up clues about the ancient city of Gath
Where—Gath
When—now (also yearly since 1996)
Why—to add to the wealth of objects already uncovered
How—through archeological excavation

Paragraph 2 tells the most important details—what diggers have found so far this season—Philistine jugs. They've also found decorations often used in Greek art. These findings help to show a link between the Philistines and the Greeks. It helps to support the theory or belief that these people originally migrated from the Aegean area.

Paragraphs 3 and 4 add background information about the Philistines, helping readers to see where and how they fit into history.

The original *News Current* article goes on for two more paragraphs. It gives more background information. Because the article used the inverted triangle organization, I was able to cut the story short without losing the most important information.

CWJ

Now it's your turn. Read this news story:

Teacher's Strike in Kenya

In September, 200,000 teachers in Kenya's National Union of teachers went on a strike that affected 10 million children.

Educators are protesting a government action that **diverted** $74 million in education funds to Kenya's military. The money had been intended for hiring more teachers.

Kenya was praised when it made public primary school free in 2003. Nearly one million children who had never been to school were enrolled. But that move led to severe overcrowding. Now as many as 50 and sometimes 100 students jam into classes with a single teacher in Kenya's public schools.

Now tell what each paragraph contains:

Paragraphs 1 and 2:
Who—
What—
When—
Where—
Why—
How—

Paragraph 3:

CAPSULE 5   1.1.5

WRITING A NEWS STORY WITH A HEADLINE

In 1.1.3, you chose an event from one of your communities and answered the 5 W's and How. You wrote a lead for your story. Today we want you to finish this story.

First, check your lead to make sure it includes the 5 W's. Make sure you've answered these questions:

1. Who is the story about?
2. What is happening in the story?
3. Where does the story take place?
4. When did the story take place?
5. Why is the event occurring?

If there's a "How" that is important to the story, make sure to answer that question in your lead too. Remember, you need to make the story interesting to hold your readers' attention. Let's say you were writing about a parade in your hometown. What angle could you take to create an interesting lead? *"A parade took place in downtown Mayberry yesterday,"* is boring. *"High winds almost caused a wreck when a float blew over during yesterday's Easter parade,"* is more interesting. The parade itself IS news. But if there's an exciting moment in the parade, that's bigger news. You want to lead with the information that is of highest interest to your reader.

The middle section of your inverted pyramid contains the most important details. If you were covering a parade, that might be how many floats there were, descriptions of some of the most interesting floats, and how many people attended.

Remember, journalistic style means using simple sentence constructions. You should be as clear as possible. This isn't the time to pull out your most flowery language. Use strong verbs, but don't get fancy. Your goal is to make your writing easy to understand.

In the tip of your inverted pyramid, you'll want to include background information. If you were writing about the parade, here's where you would give its history. How many years has the parade taken place? Who or what group founded the parade?

When you finish the article, it's time to write your headline. Remember, you need the "wow" factor here. *"Easter Parade"* won't grab most people's attention. *"Float Nearly Causes Wreck,"* will!

CWJ

IN YOUR JOURNAL ▶

Today, finish the news story you began in 1.1.3:

1. Test the lead you wrote in 1.1.3. Does it answer the 5 W's? Is there a "how" that needs to be included? If you don't have an interesting slant or angle on the story, try to find one. Rewrite the lead, including the biggest or most interesting news.
2. In the next section, include the most important details. If you attended the event, try to picture key moments in your mind and include details.

(Example: Tom and Jerry's Veterinary Office took the top prize in the float contest. The colorful float carried several real dogs and cats. On a stage at the top of the float, a paper-mache Tom chased a paper-mache Jerry in circles. A sound system played the Looney Tunes "Tom and Jerry" soundtrack.)

3.   Conclude your article with some background information.

When you've finished, read your story aloud. Did you leave out any words? Are there any parts that sound funny or don't make sense when you hear them? Make any changes necessary to make the story clear.

STYLE TIME

 Now go back through and circle all the commas. Read each sentence to the first comma. Stop. Is it a complete idea? Does it have a subject and a verb? If so, what comes after the comma? Read it aloud. Does it express a complete thought? If the answer is yes, have you included a word that links the two independent clauses—like and or but? If not, correct the comma splice by using one of the four fixes we showed you in 1.1.1.

Do the same for all sentences in your news story.

THE RIGHT WORD

Below are the five vocabulary words in context for this week. You should already have defined them in your journal as you found them in the reading.

1.   Journalism's writing style is geared toward getting information across quickly and **succinctly**.
2.   Good reporters should be **objective**.
3.   Reporters write precisely; they don't include **jargon**.
4.   As we've already said, this organization allows readers to get the most **salient** points of the story by reading the headline and the first paragraph or two.
5. Educators are protesting a government action that **diverted** $74 million in education funds to Kenya's military.

Using your thesaurus, try to find the BEST word to replace the bold word in the sentence. If you aren't familiar with the meanings of all the synonyms for each word in the thesaurus, you may need to use your dictionary to look them up. That way you can choose the word that best fits the sentence.

Write with WORLD

CAPSULE 1

1.2.1

WHY INTERVIEW?

When writing your news story for Lesson 1.1, where did you get your information? Since the assignment was to report on an event, you probably attended the event and wrote your news story based on your observations. Being an eyewitness to an event is the best case scenario for a reporter. However, a reporter can't always be there when news happens. In such cases, a reporter must rely on the next best option: the reports of eyewitnesses to the event. That includes observers and those involved in the event.

As a reporter, the best way to get the reports of eyewitnesses is to talk with them. You need to conduct an interview. An interview is a conversation in which one person questions another to gather specific information.

There are three reasons you might choose to interview a person for a news story:
1)   They participated in the event you are writing about (example: a player or coach of a basketball team)
2)   They observed the event you're writing about (example: a spectator at a basketball game)
3)   They're an expert on the event you're writing about (example: a professional basketball player or sportscaster who can offer an expert opinion on the game)

Interviewing is essential for a reporter. But it's useful in other types of writing too. For instance, you might interview a doctor when writing a research paper on head injuries in football. Or say you were writing a short story about an airplane pilot. Where better to get information than from a pilot himself?

In this lesson, we'll work on honing your interviewing skills. From deciding whom you might interview for your news story to writing questions to quoting an interview in your story, this lesson will teach you how to incorporate eyewitness and expert views into your writing.

THE PROFESSOR'S OFFICE

 Interviewing is essential for reporters who want to write pieces that are interesting and relevant. All reporters take courses that teach interview techniques, and they practice these methods on a daily basis.

But why should you care? You're not a newspaper reporter (yet!) and you don't interview people on a regular basis. How is this going to help you?

Knowing how to interview well is essential for your future success. Obviously, in this assignment, interviewing well will be key to the success of your essay. However, the interviewing lessons discussed in this capsule could have a larger impact on your life. Let me explain.

Every week, I meet with high school seniors who want to attend the university where I teach. The time we spend in my office is called a "college interview": I ask questions to learn about their interests, and they ask me questions to learn about the university.

Sometimes these interviews are a lot of fun. I love talking to students who know how to ask questions; I especially enjoy students who take over—who control—the interview. These students know what they want to learn about the university, have lots of questions, and pose follow-up questions. Their calm confidence is impressive: they are the type of student I want to teach, and many of them receive scholarships to universities because they know how to talk with adults.

Other times, these interviews can be painful—30 minutes can feel like three hours. The student barely talks, answers my questions with short, staccato sentences like "Yes. I like science." In many of these interviews parents will actually start talking for their child. Last year I asked a visiting student if they liked reading. The student answered, "Yes." I followed up with the following question: "What are some of your favorite books?" The response? "I don't have any." In 35 minutes, I asked 23 questions. We did not have a conversation, and I felt sorry for the student.

Why did the student respond so poorly? Many students never learn how to interview or to talk with adults. Knowing how to ask questions, listen intently to responses, and have long conversations with adults is an important skill.

Pay close attention to this unit on interviewing. You may feel nervous during your first interview; you may even feel like this isn't what you want to do. These feelings are normal. Challenge yourself to get better at interviewing and building conversations—you want to be the student who comfortably enters the professor's office and dazzles the professor with thoughtful questions and meaningful responses.

CWJ

In this lesson, you will add eyewitness report or expert opinion to the story you wrote in 1.1.

Today reread your news story. How might your story be improved by adding material from an interview? If your article is about a soccer game you recently watched, who could add some interesting additional information to your story? The team's coach? The player who scored the game-winning goal?

After rereading your story, make a list of at least three people who you might interview to add information and interest to your story. In two-to-three sentences, explain how this information could improve your story.

◀ IN YOUR JOURNAL

CAPSULE 2

1.2.2

WHOM SHOULD I INTERVIEW?

Last time, you made a list of potential interviewees. How do you decide which you should include in your story? This is a good time to think about your audience. If you wrote a sports story, whom do you think your audience would like to hear from? If you've ever watched ESPN or the local news, you probably have a pretty good idea. A player can hardly make it off the field before someone sticks a microphone in his face. Coaches for college and professional teams often appear at press conferences right after the game, where they answer the questions of a throng of reporters and offer opinions about what made them win or lose the game.

You should also consider what will add the most value to your story. If your article covers the opening night performance of "The Wizard of Oz" your drama club performed, it would be interesting to get some comments from audience members about what they thought of the show. However, an interview with the musical's director would offer more facts about the design and ideas behind the production. Both would add to the story, but an interview with the director probably provides more solid information that your readers can use in determining whether or not they want to see the show. When you have the opportunity to interview an expert, it's a good idea to do so. Usually that adds the most value to your story.

If you're still having trouble deciding whom you should interview, do an informal poll of parents and/ or friends. Whose opinion or comments would they be most interested in seeing quoted in your story? Remember, what is considered "news" is information people want to know. That's why concerts of the local medieval recorder society might get a line or two on the back page of the local newspaper on a slow day, but the high school's Friday night football game makes the front page of the sports section every

Saturday during football season.

Once you've decided on a subject to interview, you're ready to move on to your CWJ.

CWJ

IN YOUR JOURNAL ▶

You've decided whom you'd like to interview. Now it's time to try to make contact. Do you already know the person? If so, you or your parents may have their phone number and/or email address. If not, have your parents help you search online for the person's phone number or email address.

Once you've gotten the contact information, you need to write an email or a phone script for yourself. If you have both an email address and phone number, we advise sending an email first, then following up by telephone.

Today in your journal, practice writing an email and a phone script requesting an interview with your eyewitness or expert.

Here's a sample email to get you started:

> *Dear Coach _____,*
>
> *I attended the Fighting Eagle's championship game last night. What a game! As a student who is interested in journalism, I would love to do a short interview with you (5-10 minutes) about the game. I'm working on an article for school and any commentary you could provide on the game or the Eagle's chances at regionals would be appreciated.*
>
> *Sincerely,*
>
> *Jimmy Jackson*

If you have only a phone number, go ahead and write a script requesting an interview. But don't call yet. Often, if you actually get the interviewee on the phone, they're willing to talk with you right then. So you'll want to have your questions ready before you call.

PREPARING FOR AN INTERVIEW

 By now, you should have an interview lined up. If you haven't heard back from your first choice, you may want to move on to the next candidate on your list. As a reporter, you have to get news out quickly. Being flexible and willing to change plans to get the story out on time is often necessary.

Before you call, be prepared. You should write down three or four questions. Since your article is short, you only need one or two quotes from your source. By having three or four questions ready, you should produce plenty of material to choose from.

What kinds of questions should you ask? Start with your interests. If you were reading the story, what would you want to know? **Jot** down at least two questions. If I were interviewing the coach of the Fighting Eagles, I might ask one question about the previous game and one about the upcoming regional game:

1)   Your team was trailing in the first half of last night's game. They really picked it up in the second half and came back for the win. What spurred them on to victory?

2)   You have a young team—mostly sophomores. How do you think they will stand up to the pressure of regionals this weekend?

Now check your questions. Make sure they can't be answered with "yes," or "no." You won't have a quote for your story unless you ask questions that require more detailed answers. If you're having trouble, grab a newspaper or look at one online. Examine stories that are similar to the type you're writing. The stories won't include the reporter's questions. But read the quotes. What questions might the reporter have asked to get the quote in the story? The same exact question may not work for your story, but reading a few might give you some ideas.

After you develop your questions, you need to decide how you will record them. If you're doing an in-person interview, take a voice recorder if you have one. It's also possible to record a phone interview using a cell phone, your computer, or equipment that attaches to your phone. If you DO use a recorder either in person or by telephone, you must ask the interviewee for permission to record the interview. Recording a conversation without permission is illegal in some states.

If you can't record the interview, you'll need to write down answers. Write as fast as you can, and read the quote back to the person you're interviewing when finished. You want to make sure you've accurately represented what he or she said.

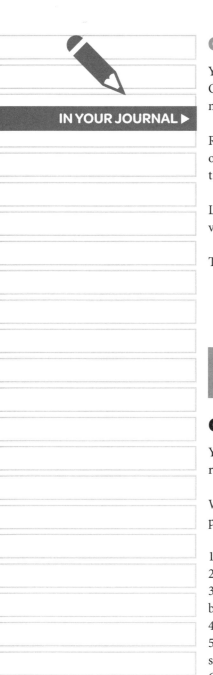

CWJ

You should have developed at least two questions in today's capsule. Come up with one or two more. Once you have your questions ready, run them by a parent or teacher. See if they have any suggestions for making them clearer or more focused.

Record your questions in your journal. Then write them on another sheet of paper. List them in the order of importance, beginning with the one you'd most like an answer to. That way if the interview goes off track, your most important question gets answered.

Leave plenty of space to write answers on the paper as you interview. Even if you plan to record the interview, it's a good idea to take notes as a backup in case your recorder doesn't work.

That's it! You're done for today.

CAPSULE 4
1.2.4

CONTROLLING THE INTERVIEW

You've got an interview scheduled. You've got questions. You've got a way to record your interview. You're ready!

Whether you are interviewing over the phone or in person, make sure you are polite. If interviewing by phone:

1. Call promptly at the scheduled time.
2. Introduce yourself: "Hi, Coach Collins. This is Jimmy Jackson."
3. Thank the interviewee for agreeing to the interview. "Thanks for agreeing to talk with me about the basketball team. The interview shouldn't take long—five minutes or so."
4. Ask permission to record. "Is it okay if I record you so that I can quote you accurately in my story?"
5. If you're interviewing a professional, ask for their exact title. For each person you interview, make sure you are spelling their name correctly and using the name they prefer. "Do you prefer to be quoted as Coach Don Collins or Coach Donald Collins?"

From there, you should launch into your questions. For an in-person interview, the script looks almost the same:

1. Arrive a few minutes before your scheduled meeting.
2. Introduce yourself: "Hi, Coach Collins. I'm Jimmy Johnson."
3. Shake hands.
4. Thank him for agreeing to the interview. "Thanks for agreeing to talk with me about the basketball team. The interview shouldn't take long—five minutes or so."
5. Ask permission to record. "Is it okay if I record you so that I can quote you accurately in my story?"
6. If you're interviewing a professional, ask for their exact title. For each person you interview, make sure you are spelling their name correctly and using the name they prefer. "Do you prefer to be quoted as Coach Don Collins or Coach Donald Collins?"

After you've asked your questions and the interview is finished, thank the interviewee again for taking the time to talk with you. They may ask to see a copy of your story when it's finished. If so, get an email address so that you can send the story.

Having questions is essential to being prepared for an interview, and generally you want to get those questions answered. But sometimes, what the interviewee says will make you think of another question. Don't be too tied to the questions you came with. If the interview takes an unexpected, interesting turn, that's okay. The best interviews are NOT the ones where you're so glued to your questions that you don't really even listen to the answers. The best interviews turn into conversations.

That being said, sometimes your interview goes completely off the rails into a topic that isn't really what you're writing about. If what the interviewee is saying doesn't help you, continue to listen politely. At the first opportunity, when he finishes his answer, ask another question from your list.

When your questions are answered or your time is up, end the interview with a thank you and another handshake in person, or a thank you over the phone.

WORLD WISDOM

Getting a good interview can make or break a story. But as *WORLD Magazine* reporter Edward Lee Pitts reminds us, we must never put the desire to write a good story above the needs of the person we're interviewing. We must see them as real people, not just good quotes.

Joining a U.S. Army unit in Iraq as a reporter had its challenges. Soldiers would come up to me pointing at their uniforms and ask:

"You're not wearing one of these? Why are you here?"

But I began to understand why the soldiers got so tense around reporters one day after a deadly battle. The unit involved in the firefight came back to the base with sullen faces and blood on their uniforms. They had lost one of their own.

But before they could even reach their rooms to mourn in private, a pack of reporters surrounded them. Sticking recorders and notebooks into the faces of the troops, these reporters barked a barrage of questions at the still stunned soldiers. Many of the soldiers brushed them off. Surveying the scene from a few steps away, I instinctively tucked my own reporter's notebook into my pants pocket. I saw one of the sergeants leaned up against a wall, eyes downcast, his feet kicking the Iraqi desert dust. I went up to him, leaned against the same wall and said that, as an American, I was sorry for his loss. There was a pause, and then he said:

"It should not have happened that way."

"What do you mean," I asked, my notebook still hidden in my pocket.

He began to recount the battle. After a couple of minutes, I gently interrupted him and asked if I could write this down. I told him that it might be one small way to honor his friend by telling the story of his sacrifice. He said sure. So I pulled out my notebook and began to take notes.

I learned that day that as a reporter we should never forget our humanity. When we go to places to tell stories, often interviewing people who have been through something tragic, we should remember to treat others as we would like for ourselves to be treated.

Addressing somebody as a person first and a story subject second is not only the right thing to do, it also allows whomever you are interviewing to feel the most comfortable while answering your questions.

Not long after I pulled out my notebook in front of that sergeant back in Iraq, I found myself inside a soldier's room. Troops who had survived that battle surrounded me still wearing their soiled uniforms. They told me all sorts of details about the battle. I could tell that it made them feel a little better talking about what they had been through. So I kept asking questions. I was the only reporter that day invited to the room, and it's probably because I kept my notebook in my pocket first.

Helpful hint: Once you're prepared for the interview, ask a parent to role-play the interview with you. Practice introducing yourself, shaking hands, and taking notes. Have them try to take you off topic so that you can practice controlling the interview. Practice enough times that you feel ready for the interview, confident that you can present yourself professionally and politely.

CWJ

IN YOUR JOURNAL ▶

Once you've finished your interview, if it's recorded, you'll need to **transcribe** it. In your journal today, transcribe the recording. You may have to listen to each section several times to ensure accuracy. You don't have to transcribe every word—just the sections you are considering adding to your story.

If you wrote the answers by hand, as soon as you get home, rewrite them in your journal. It's likely that you used some sort of shorthand or wrote messily if you were writing fast. The sooner you rewrite the answers, the better you'll remember your own shorthand and/or recognize what you wrote.

CAPSULE 5

1.2.5

INCORPORATING DIRECT AND INDIRECT QUOTES

In your CWJ last time, you transcribed your interview. Today, you will **incorporate** material from your interview into your news story. We'd like for you to find two quotes from your interview that you believe would add interest and important information to your story. Read back through your CWJ entry, marking your two best quotes (highlight, underline, or star them.)

CHOOSING QUOTES

Now read back through your article. Can you see a spot where the quotes you've chosen would fit in? For instance, if you were writing about the Fighting Eagles' sectional game, a quote about Hank Pittman's buzzer shot might go right after you describe it in your article:

At the last second, point guard Hank Pittman threw the ball from the half-court line. The ball hit the backboard. The gym fell silent as the ball slowly rolled around the rim. As it swished through the hoop, the crowd exploded with screams and applause.

"I was holding my breath till I saw it drop through the hoop," said Hank Pittman, the team's leading scorer and the only senior in the starting lineup. "The next thing I knew, my teammates had picked me up and were carrying me off the floor."

Another quote—one about the team's prospects at regionals, might go at the end of the story:

Pittman said he's excited about regionals. "We're going to go out there and play our hardest. We'd love to make it to state this year."

If you're having a hard time finding a spot for the quote, look back through your transcript. Is there a quote that fits your story better? If so, use that one instead.

IDENTIFYING QUOTES

Look back over the quotes by Hank Pittman in the example article. Notice the tags that tell who is being quoted. The first time you introduce someone in a news story, you need to identify them for readers. Who is this person? Why are you quoting them? Give a little one-sentence background:

"We're ready for regionals," said Donald Collins, Putnam County High School's senior coach. "These boys have worked incredibly hard this season, and they've really improved."

In **subsequent** quotes, you just need to identify the person being quoted by last name (and title if they have one):
"We hope to have a big crowd there for regionals," said Coach Pittman.

INDIRECT QUOTES

Sometimes it's best to **paraphrase** a source. Why would you do so? If you're not exactly sure what they said, you shouldn't put it in quotes. It's dishonest. It's tempting sometimes to want to put words in someone's mouth. By just changing what they said a little, it would sound so much better! But that's not right. When you put something inside quotes, you're telling your readers, "This is exactly what my source said."

Newspaper quotes are typically short—a sentence or two. However, if your source gives good information that you would like to include, you might paraphrase so that you can fit it in.

Here's an example:
Coach Collins said he thinks the team can win at regionals.

Sometimes you might follow up an indirect quote with a direct quote:
Coach Collins said he thinks the team can win at regionals. "We've got the best team we've had in at least 10 years. I think these boys can win on Friday if they go out there and play their best."

Using an indirect quote to summarize helps to keep you from quoting too much. A key quote or two adds to the story. But when overused, they lose their effectiveness.

When you think you've figured out what information you want to add, move on to your CWJ for today.

CWJ

IN YOUR JOURNAL ▶

Today, you should add two quotes to your story. At least one should be a direct quote.

1.   Rewrite your story to include your quotes. If you drafted on the computer, this should be fairly easy. Remember, when quoting, each time you have a new speaker you begin a new paragraph. Newspaper paragraphs are also short. It's likely that the quote and its tag will make an entirely new paragraph.

2.   Once you've added your quotes, check your tags. Have you accurately and adequately introduced the source (or sources) that you interviewed?

3.   Read your article aloud. Does the quoted material add information and interest to your story? Does it fit where you placed it in the story?

STYLE TIME

Using quotation marks is easy. There's one basic rule: All punctuation marks go inside the quotes. Of course, there are a couple of exceptions. But they really don't apply when you are quoting people speaking, which is what we're working on in this lesson.

Here are a couple of other tips to help you out:

1.   If you use a tag *before* your quote, the period (or question mark or exclamation mark) at the end of the quote ends the sentence. You don't need two.
Example:
Coach Brown said, "We're excited about the game."

2.   If you use a tag *after* your quote, your quoted sentence will end with a comma inside the quotes instead of a period.
Example:
"We're excited about the game," Coach Brown said.

3.   If you use other punctuation besides a period for your quoted sentence, put it *before* the quotation marks. You will also have a period at the end of the entire sentence/tag combination.
Example:
"We're excited about the game!" Coach Brown said.

So here's a quick recap:
▶   Commas go inside quotes.
▶   Periods go inside quotes.
▶   Exclamation marks go inside quotes.
▶   Question marks go inside quotes.

Now check back thorough your story, circling all quotation marks. Do you have anything that looks like this?

1.   ",   If so, change to this: ,"
2.   ".   If so, change to this: ."
3.   "!   If so, change to this: !"
4.   "?   If so, change to this: ?"

THE RIGHT WORD

 Below are the five vocabulary words in context for this week. You should already have defined them in your journal as you found them in the reading.

1. **Jot** down at least two questions.
2. Once you've finished your interview, if it's recorded, you'll need to **transcribe** it.
3. Today, you will **incorporate** material from your interview into your news story.
4. In **subsequent** quotes, you just need to identify the person being quoted by last name (and title if they have one).
5. Sometimes it's best to **paraphrase** a source.

Using your thesaurus, try to find the BEST word to replace the bold word in the sentence. If you aren't familiar with the meanings of all the synonyms for each word in the thesaurus, you may need to use your dictionary to look them up. That way you can choose the word that best fits the sentence.

Write with WORLD

UNIT 1 / LESSON 3

REPORTING AND INTERPRETING

WORKING WITH CONTROVERSY

CAPSULE 1

1.3.1

WHAT IS CONTROVERSY?

Some people might define a controversy as an argument. Technically, that's a possible definition. However, most of the time when we say a subject, activity, or idea creates controversy, we're talking about more than a simple argument. *The Merriam-Webster Dictionary* says that a controversy is "a discussion marked especially by the expression of opposing views." We would take that definition one step further to describe what people usually mean when they say a topic is controversial. A topic, activity, or idea is controversial if people disagree and there is conflicting evidence suggesting that either side might have the stronger point.

Here's an example:
Playing elite-level sports is good/bad for middle-school aged children.

If you were to look up this topic, you would find persuasive arguments on both sides of the issue. Some families have seen their children learn a strong work ethic, gain coordination and skill, learn to enjoy sports, and even earn college scholarships through being on a select or elite sports team. Others have had the opposite experience. Their children have developed repetitive motion injuries from overtraining, have missed out on other social and athletic opportunities because of the grueling schedule, and have become burned out on the sport in a short time.

People—especially those who have experienced the negatives or positives of elite teams—have strong opinions about this topic. When your parents were kids, elite sports was hardly an issue. But in recent years, more and more elite teams have sprung up. And with the growing trend, the topic has become more controversial. A controversial topic, then, is any topic upon which people disagree and there isn't **incontrovertible** evidence that supports one side or the other.

In this lesson, you'll begin looking for a controversial topic that interests you and connects to your life in some way. In the next lesson, you'll write a feature article on that topic.

A word of caution: There are some topics many people consider controversial but are not controversial for Christians. For instance, the Bible is clear on the sanctity of life. Old Testament law requires death for those who shed innocent blood (Exodus 20:12). Jesus speaks of the value of human life in the New Testament (Matthew 10:29-31). Topics like abortion or intentionally taking the lives of the elderly or sick are not controversial for us. No matter what "evidence" people might offer, the Bible is always our authority on moral issues.

We don't want you to choose a topic that the Bible gives a clear answer on—for you, that's not a controversial topic. We want you to explore a topic with two sides you can truly consider. It's fine if you've already formed an opinion. However, we will want you to consider both sides of the topic and write a feature that is as unbiased as possible.

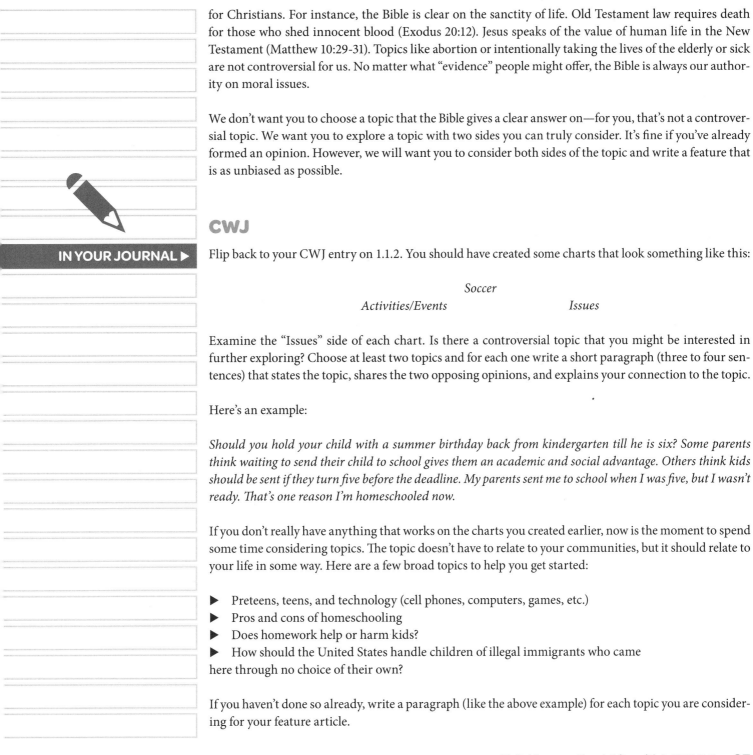

IN YOUR JOURNAL ▶

CWJ

Flip back to your CWJ entry on 1.1.2. You should have created some charts that look something like this:

Soccer

Activities/Events	*Issues*

Examine the "Issues" side of each chart. Is there a controversial topic that you might be interested in further exploring? Choose at least two topics and for each one write a short paragraph (three to four sentences) that states the topic, shares the two opposing opinions, and explains your connection to the topic.

Here's an example:

Should you hold your child with a summer birthday back from kindergarten till he is six? Some parents think waiting to send their child to school gives them an academic and social advantage. Others think kids should be sent if they turn five before the deadline. My parents sent me to school when I was five, but I wasn't ready. That's one reason I'm homeschooled now.

If you don't really have anything that works on the charts you created earlier, now is the moment to spend some time considering topics. The topic doesn't have to relate to your communities, but it should relate to your life in some way. Here are a few broad topics to help you get started:

▶ Preteens, teens, and technology (cell phones, computers, games, etc.)
▶ Pros and cons of homeschooling
▶ Does homework help or harm kids?
▶ How should the United States handle children of illegal immigrants who came here through no choice of their own?

If you haven't done so already, write a paragraph (like the above example) for each topic you are considering for your feature article.

CAPSULE 2

FACT VERSUS OPINION

In this lesson and the next, you will be both reading and writing news. Before we go any further, it's a good idea to take a moment to think about facts—and how opinion and bias can creep into our reporting if we're not careful. Doing so will also help you recognize the ways opinions and biases can sneak into the news you read.

Every reporter comes to each story with opinions and a worldview. Even when a writer is trying to be perfectly fair and unbiased, it's nearly impossible for a writer's beliefs or opinions not to show up somewhere in a story.

Statistics: Numbers are always facts, right? Yes—and no. Writers can slip opinions into seemingly cold, hard facts. Let's say a reporter likes a certain politician. The reporter could say, "Nearly 1,000 people crowded into a town hall meeting to hear Senator Smith's speech." If he didn't like Senator Smith, he might say, "Only 900 people showed up to hear Senator Smith speak."

Word Choice: Opinions can be hidden in the types of words a reporter uses. Does the reporter have a negative or positive attitude toward his subject? Calling a country's leader a dictator conveys a much different image than saying he's a socialist—though both may be accurate titles.

Journalistic Ventriloquism: Reporters generally are not allowed to offer their own opinions in a news story. But they can—and do—give their opinions by finding someone to interview who holds the same opinion on the topic as they do. When that interviewee says what the journalist wants readers to hear, he or she puts it in the story as a quote. For instance, a reporter who favors gun control might interview a parent whose child was accidentally shot and injured. A reporter against gun control might interview a person who used a gun to successfully ward off an intruder.

Photographs: Reporters can choose pictures that influence reader opinions. If a story about a presidential candidate runs under a pleasant, smiling picture, it might subconsciously give the readers pleasant feelings about him. Choosing another image where the same candidate is frowning or looks angry may have the opposite effect.

Story Choice: Even if a story is as objective as humanly possible, it still displays an opinion. The fact that a story appears in a paper at all offers the opinion that the story is news. For instance, when a newspaper chooses to cover a story on the high school's new gymnasium but fails to cover the opening of a new branch of the city's library, the paper is offering an opinion on which one of the two events is more interesting or more important.

As both a reader and writer of news stories, use these examples of how fact can be infused with opinion to help you detect—and work to avoid—bias.

CWJ

Read back through the news story you wrote for Lesson 1.1 and revised for Lesson 1.2. List any examples you find where you've inserted your own opinion into the story. Look especially for examples of biased word choice and journalistic ventriloquism.

CAPSULE 3   1.3.3

DON'T RUSH TO JUDGMENT

WORLD WISDOM

WORLD Magazine Editor Mindy Belz warns of the dangers of rushing to judgment—even when the evidence seems clear.

Ever been accused of something you didn't do? Ever accused someone else and learned it was all a misunderstanding? We've all probably been in both places, and it's no fun. But the lessons learned in those circumstances are valuable for journalists: Reserve judgment.

For journalists, the consequences of failing to show good judgment can be serious. To be purposefully wrong in public will damage your own integrity, but also the reputation of the one who is wronged in the process. That's why it's important for writers and editors to have accountability with one another, to ask hard and probing questions, and to not let deadlines—or headlines—become more important than the truth.

Consider this case: A prominent public official is accused of stealing money. The money is gone, and he is someone who had access to it. In fact, there are photos of him talking with the young woman who has keys to the vault. The expression on his face suggests he is asking her for something. Later he is driving around town in a new luxury car, and taking his wife on vacation in the Bahamas. What could be more clear?

Perhaps this man does not have the best reputation. Even though he denies stealing the money, newshounds everywhere want to run a story about the crime he may have committed, with the suggestive photos. Let the readers sort it out, they say. But it's better to wait and investigate diligently, seeking the truth before publicizing a sensational story. Remember Haman, the king's officer? The book of Esther tells us he built gallows on which to hang Mordecai the Jew and tried to accuse him of a crime. When the king discovered that Haman was the criminal, not Mordecai, Haman was hanged on the very gallows he had built.

Today we'll look at a real-life example of how a rush to judgment by the media sometimes causes damage that can never be undone.

On July 27, 1996, crowds filled Centennial Olympic Park in Atlanta, Georgia, a gathering place for those attending the Summer Olympics. Thousands were there, though it was after midnight. Unnoticed, someone had left a green backpack underneath a bench. Security guard Richard Jewell discovered the bag and alerted Georgia Bureau of Investigation officers. Jewell and other security officers began clearing the area so that a bomb squad could examine the suspicious backpack. Just a few minutes later, the backpack exploded. One woman, Alice Hawthorne, was killed. Over one hundred others were injured. But if Richard Jewell had not been alert and noticed the package, many more may have been injured or killed in the crowded park.

At least, that's what newspapers said at first. Jewell was treated as a hero. Soon though, newspapers began reporting that Jewell was a possible suspect in the case. It seemed some of the journalists had decided he was guilty. They searched for facts about his life that supported this opinion—facts that matched those of FBI profiles of lone bomber types. Many news agencies wrote stories that suggested he might have planted the bomb so he could find it, making him look like a hero.

The Atlanta Journal-Constitution went so far as to say that Jewell "fit the profile of a lone bomber." The media **frenzy** surrounding Jewell made many people rush to judgment, assuming he had committed the crime. But the evidence didn't add up. By October of that year, the FBI formally cleared him of the crime. Eric Rudolph, a lone bomber responsible for a series of bombings, eventually confessed to the crime.

Richard Jewell's "trial by media" tarnished his good name. He actually was a hero. A rush to judgment by the media created employment difficulties for Mr. Jewell and made him a villain in the eyes of many readers. He eventually sued many of the media outlets who had **libeled** him in their stories. However, the **notoriety** of his assumed role in the bombing for those few months haunted him for the rest of his life.

Beginning in the next capsule, you'll examine an issue. The story of Richard Jewell is a good reminder that just because the evidence seems to point in a particular direction, you shouldn't rush to judgment. Proverbs 18:13 says, "To answer before listening is a folly and a shame." As Christians, we need to be particularly careful to withhold judgment until we gather as many facts as we can.

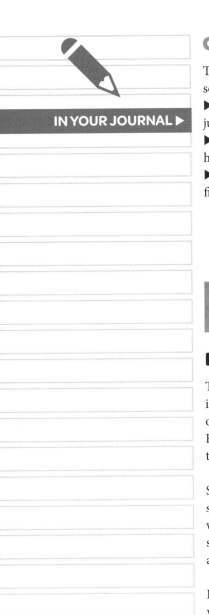

Think of a time when you've rushed to judgment and write a paragraph about it in your journal. Here are some ideas to get you started:

▶ Have you ever met a person and immediately formed a negative opinion, only to later find that your judgment was inaccurate?

▶ Have you ever accused someone of an action that you later discovered they did not commit? (If you have brothers and sisters, this has probably happened at least once or twice!)

▶ Have you ever gone somewhere (camp, a new class or activity, a different country) and disliked it at first but changed your opinion as time went on?

CAPSULE 4
1.3.4

EXPLORING CONTROVERSIAL TOPICS

Today, we want you to explore two of the topics you listed in 1.3.1. Look back at your list. Which ones interest you the most? With a parent or teacher's help, we'd like for you to begin exploring your topic online. The goal is to find at least two newspaper articles or other reliable sources that address each topic. For each topic, one article should cast the topic in a favorable light and the other should look at the negatives, or each article should consider pros and cons.

So where should you begin? Our recommendation would be to begin with news sites. Most allow you to search exclusively for news stories. In searching the topic of whether elite sports harm or benefit children, we put the keywords "kids elite sports" into CNN's website. We found two articles quite quickly. News sites are good because they weed out many items that are not news. However, they also tend to bring up anything to do with ONE of the key words, so you get a lot of articles that don't match your exact search.

If you have any hits that seem like good sources, skim through them. Do they use any other terms for your topic that might help **refine** your search? For instance, instead of "kids elite sports," you might search again using "kids club sports." If you're still having trouble finding enough information, think about other words that relate. "Repetitive motion injury" is a problem that has escalated because of kids' overtraining, so you might use this term to help you search.

Once you feel you've exhausted the news sites, very cautiously move on to a search engine on the Internet like Google, Yahoo, Bing, or AOL. Try your key words again. Beware—much of what you find may be people's opinions, blogs, or even advertisements. For instance, when we type in "kids elite sports," we get a list of websites for companies or clubs that offer elite sports for children. They are going to be biased in favor of elite sports—because their businesses depend on kids playing on their teams!

With a parent or teacher's help, look for reputable sources. Along with respected newspapers, other good sources on the topic of kids' elite sports might be college coaches, doctors, hospitals, and the American Academy of Pediatrics, an organization made up of 60,000 pediatricians (doctors specializing in children's health).

Print out or bookmark three to four sources for each of your topics, making sure to include both negative and positive materials on the topic.

CWJ

Today, we want you to read through the sources you saved or printed on your topic. After you've finished reading, answer these questions:

1. What is one thing you learned about topic 1 that you hadn't considered before?
2. What is one thing you learned about topic 2 that you hadn't considered before?
3. Which topic do you find most interesting?
4. Which do you think you will write your feature article about?
5. Why?

◄ IN YOUR JOURNAL

CAPSULE 5

1.3.5

WHOM SHOULD I INTERVIEW?

Once you've decided on your topic, you should begin considering whom you would like to interview. You'll remember that we asked that you choose a topic that relates to you in some way. If you did so, you should know someone who is connected to the topic. For instance, if you decided to look at positives and negatives of homeschooling, you might choose to speak to a student who has experienced both a traditional classroom and a homeschool environment. Or, for an expert opinion, you might interview an educator who has spent time in a traditional classroom and has homeschooled her children as well.

If you're having trouble thinking of someone, look at the articles you gathered for 1.3.4. They include information on your topic, but they probably raise some questions as well. For instance, a story on the advantages of homeschooling may lack day-to-day details of how a parent actually homeschools. That's interesting information that helps to put a face on the topic.

Features take a more in-depth look at an issue than regular news stories do. Often, some of the extra length is used to show readers what the issue means to real, live people. That's one way you can use an interview in your feature—to humanize the issue.

Another way you can use an interview is to add expertise. If we were reading a feature about elite sports teams for kids, we'd be interested to know what an orthopedist (bone doctor) thought was the right age for kids to begin playing year-round sports. Another expert source that could shed some light on the issue would be a college coach. We'd like to know whether most of his athletes came from elite sports teams, and whether or not he found that to be an advantage.

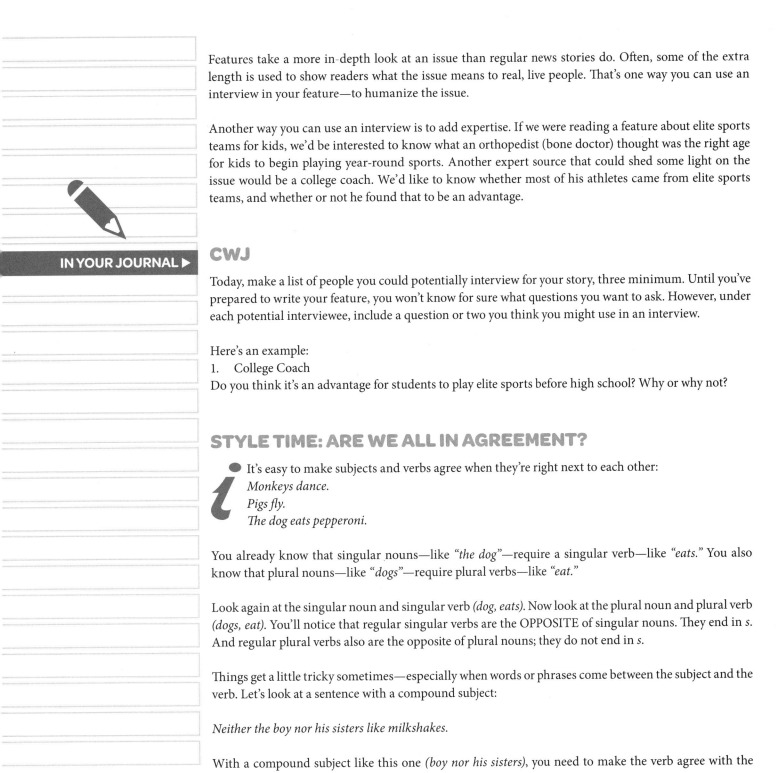

IN YOUR JOURNAL ▶

CWJ

Today, make a list of people you could potentially interview for your story, three minimum. Until you've prepared to write your feature, you won't know for sure what questions you want to ask. However, under each potential interviewee, include a question or two you think you might use in an interview.

Here's an example:
1. College Coach
Do you think it's an advantage for students to play elite sports before high school? Why or why not?

STYLE TIME: ARE WE ALL IN AGREEMENT?

It's easy to make subjects and verbs agree when they're right next to each other:
Monkeys dance.
Pigs fly.
The dog eats pepperoni.

You already know that singular nouns—like *"the dog"*—require a singular verb—like *"eats."* You also know that plural nouns—like *"dogs"*—require plural verbs—like *"eat."*

Look again at the singular noun and singular verb *(dog, eats)*. Now look at the plural noun and plural verb *(dogs, eat)*. You'll notice that regular singular verbs are the OPPOSITE of singular nouns. They end in *s.* And regular plural verbs also are the opposite of plural nouns; they do not end in *s.*

Things get a little tricky sometimes—especially when words or phrases come between the subject and the verb. Let's look at a sentence with a compound subject:

Neither the boy nor his sisters like milkshakes.

With a compound subject like this one *(boy nor his sisters)*, you need to make the verb agree with the noun closest to the verb. In this instance, *like* is the closest to *sisters*.

However, what happens when you have two singular nouns? Let's look at this sentence:

The boy and girl hate broccoli.

Two singular nouns make a plural subject when joined by *"and."* So *boy and girl* require a plural verb *(hate)*.

One word, however, can make a big difference. Change *and* to *or* and we have a new rule. Here's an example:

Some boy or girl in this class likes chocolate!

When joined by *"or,"* both subjects remain singular—they don't join to create a plural subject. As a result, the verb is singular *(likes)*.

Other tricky words and situations for which you should be on the lookout include:
The news is good. (looks plural but is singular)
The class is buying a gift for the teacher. (collective noun—all the people in the class make up a single group)

You get the idea. After you write your feature, we'll test it out for subject-verb agreement.

THE RIGHT WORD

 Below are the five vocabulary words in context for this week. You should already have defined them in your journal as you found them in the reading.

1. A controversial topic, then, is any topic upon which people disagree and there isn't **incontrovertible** evidence that supports one side or the other.
2. The media **frenzy** surrounding Jewell made many people rush to judgment, assuming he had committed the crime.
3. He eventually sued many of the media outlets who **libeled** him in their stories.
4. However, the **notoriety** of his assumed role in the bombing for those few months haunted him for the rest of his life.
5. Do they use any other terms for your topic that might help **refine** your search?

Using your thesaurus, try to find the BEST word to replace the bold word in the sentence. If you aren't familiar with the meanings of all the synonyms for each word in the thesaurus, you may need to use your dictionary to look them up. That way you can choose the word that best fits the sentence.

Write with WORLD

CAPSULE 1

1.4.1

WHAT IS A FEATURE ARTICLE?

 In 1.1, you wrote a news story. You used the inverted pyramid method to get the most important facts across as quickly as possible. That's the purpose of most news stories—to supply key information in a few hundred words or less.

But most newspapers and magazines also regularly include feature articles. These articles go beyond briefly enumerating key facts. They take a more in-depth look at an issue. Features can take a wide variety of forms. Some of the most popular include:

Profiles: A newspaper might profile a popular performer, a politician, or even a group of people they believe their community would like to know more about. Typically, the journalist would interview the person or group being profiled to provide detailed information and quotes.

Embedded journalist: A newspaper or television news show might send a reporter to experience a way of life unfamiliar to many readers. For instance, reporters have sometimes gone to stay with members of the military so that they can report on the details of soldiers' daily life. They've done the same with homeless shelters, public housing, schools, and many other environments. (See Edward Lee Pitt's WORLD Wisdom in 1.2 where he shares his experience as an embedded journalist.)

"How-to" features: Informative features give readers directions on everything from how to find a good doctor to how to build a doghouse. These sometimes follow trends—perhaps telling readers what colors and styles of clothing are popular or how to spend less on groceries in a weak economy. They don't necessarily tie to a news story, but they provide information that the media believes readers want or need to know.

News Feature: These articles often cover "hard news"—stories that are currently making headlines. A news feature takes a more in-depth look at the story, examining various angles. They involve more research and often will include multiple interviews. News magazines such as *WORLD* which are published weekly or bi-weekly include many feature-length articles in each issue.

"Trend" feature: This type of news story covers a topic—often a controversial one. It may be a rising movement in popular culture, a new fashion, or even more significant change. Topics that trace trends might focus on how smart phones have changed our lives, how we practice our faith as compared to people a generation ago, or how a pop icon's hairstyle and clothing choices have influenced teens' and tweens' sense of style.

As you can see, part of the fun of a feature is that there's a wide variety of choice when it comes to the topic. The structure is different than a regular news story, too. A feature is organized more like the narratives you've written—it doesn't utilize the inverted pyramid. You'll want an introduction that grabs your readers' attention. The body will lay out the information you want to provide readers. And the conclusion should wrap the story up in some way. You could circle back to what you began with—or end with a quote that either wraps the story up or leaves the reader with something to think about.

For the feature you'll write in this lesson, we'd like you to work on either a news feature or a trend feature. While some newspapers and magazines include opinions, we'd like your feature to be informational. Try to present all sides of the controversial issue you chose in the last lesson as fairly as possible.

The best way to learn to write features is to read them. *God's World News* magazines include feature articles each month. The more features you read, the better you will understand their structure.

We've included two from *Trak* to get you started. Read the articles "National Treasure Hunting" and "Digging Gold." As you read, note how the writers have incorporated more than one viewpoint as well as quotes from sources.

National Treasure Hunting

Trader Joe's, the specialty grocery chain, might not have the cheapest toilet paper or the most kinds of ketchup, but it knows how to hook customers: mango butter and cilantro-and jalapeno hummus, that's how.

While these goodies aren't on most grocery lists, they often tempt shoppers into an impulse buy. At a time when families are watching dollars, and the Web makes discount-hunting easy, unexpected treasures are an increasingly important strategy for stores.

"It's the wow factor that's getting people to buy," say Wall Street analyst Brian Sozzi.

So shoppers head into T.J. Maxx or a DSW shoe store looking for a bargain on something they need but end up splurging on bargain Ray-Bans or halfpriced Puma sneakers.

And tucked among hulking pallets of mayonnaise at Costco is an area where shoppers never know what they'll find. The hunt is on.

Costco has used the term "treasure hunt" for years to explain why up to 20% of its stock is limited-quantity items.

That treasure hunt strategy can pay. Revenue at U.S. Costco stores open at least a year was up 10% last quarter from 2010, with strong growth in non-essentials like jewelry and home and garden.

Walmart, on the other hand, is still trying to correct itself after a move to pare down to the basics—the opposite of the treasure hunt approach—proved unsuccessful.

Online competition is stinging superstores like Kmart and Walmart. Any massmarket product—think Jif peanut butter or Hanes T-shirts—can be comparison priced online, and people tend to buy from the cheapest source. Increasingly, that's Amazon.com or another Web retailer.

Meanwhile, so-called off -price stores, such as T.J. Maxx and Marshalls, pick up discontinued products and sell them cheaply. Shoppers probably won't find them for less—or at all—online.

Dollar Tree has taken the opposite approach from Walmart, expanding its assortment of "fun" discretionary products and adding more brand names. That means more surprises to tempt shoppers.

They lure customers with rockbottom prices on cleaning supplies, then ensnare them with extras like leather iPod cases.

Dollar Tree's revenue at stores open at least a year was up recently. Both traffic and the size of the average transaction increased.

TJX Cos., parent company to T.J. Maxx and other chains selling discount designer goods, gained momentum when frugality came into style. When the economy tanked, TJX began cycling inventory through its stores faster than ever, and their growth has continued at a time plagued by high gas prices and stagnant incomes.

Constantly cycling fresh merchandise is critical as the Web makes it harder for stores to compete on price. Surprises create suspense and encourage repeat visits.

And quick turnover creates a sense of false urgency: If you don't buy it today, it may not be there tomorrow.

Shoppers enjoy the competitive aspect of discount shopping, too, finding bargains other people have missed.

At DSW shoe stores, a savvy shopper digging through the clearance section might find Cole Haan snakeskin pumps for half off or white Converse All-Stars for $30.

Additionally, when shoppers find treasures, they want to share them. In the social media age, peppering shelves with unexpected finds generates free publicity through tweets or Facebook posts. Consumers marketing for retailers: a marketer's dream come true.

Trader Joe's is built almost entirely on the treasure hunt. Shopping there is "almost a thrill-seeking experience" say retail consultants—very different from major food chains, which often stock the same old same old. And because Trader Joe's prices are low, customers don't feel guilty trying new things.

By embracing the treasure hunt, many stores have been able to keep the shoppers they've attracted during the recession.

Consumers love the challenge and fun associated with discount shopping. (An occasional chocolate-covered pomegranate seed doesn't hurt either.)

But combine shoppers' discontentment problems, impulse-buying whims and overspending urges, and the treasure hunt obsession can quickly become a nightmare. —*by Kim Stegall with reporting by Associated Press*

PHOTOS:AP

Digging gold

THERE ARE SO MANY CUSTOMERS AT THE GOLD STANDARD, a New York company that buys jewelry, that it feels like Christmas. And Uncle Ben's Pawn Shop in Cleveland, Ohio, has never seen business like this.

Welcome to the new American gold rush. The price of gold is on a remarkable run, setting a record nearly every other day. Stomach-churning volatility in the stock market this month has only made investors even more gold hungry.

Some people desire gold as a safe investment for turbulent times. But what worries some investors is that others are buying gold simply because the price is rising, and they want to make money fast.

In October 2007, gold sold for about $740 an ounce. A little over a year later, it rose above $1,000 for the first time. This past March, it began rocketing up. Recently it traded for a record $1,921.

Meanwhile, stocks, despite rising sharply in the last two and a half years, are only slightly higher in price than they were a decade ago.

Gold hits a sweet spot among the elements: It's rare, but not too rare. It's chemically stable; all the gold ever mined is still around (somewhere). And it can be divided into small amounts without losing its properties.

Ultimately, though, gold is valuable because we all agree it is. It was used around the world as a currency for thousands of years, and then it gave value to paper currencies for centuries more.

Now, in a time of turmoil, from the credit downgrade and raising the debt limit in the U.S. to the growing financial crisis in Europe, gold is dazzling investors.

Since the financial crisis in 2008, world banks have bought gold as insurance against foreign currency holdings.

"Gold is the reciprocal of the world's faith in the world's central banks," says Jim Grant, editor of Grant's Interest Rate Observer, and right now, "the world is in a pickle."

Gold prices will probably keep rising until the U.S. and Europe get their finances in order, says Grant. And he doesn't expect that to happen soon. He predicts inflation will soar, further eroding the value of the dollar and leaving gold as the only good investment.

Cetin Ciner, a professor of finance at the University of North Carolina-Wilmington, disagrees. He thinks gold is near a peak, and people who buy now are blindly chasing the rising price.

Both Ciner and Grant caution, however, that when it comes to gold prices, no one really knows: You only make money if the price goes up.

Whether or not prices climb, people are deciding it's a good time to sell grandma's jewelry. Pawn shops and gold brokers report a surge of people cashing in gold.

In the past two years, Uncle Ben's owner Lou Tansky says gold sales have doubled or tripled. That figure actually masks how important gold is right now, he says, because others who would have come to his store have gone instead to unlicensed brokers that are trying to cash in.

"I saw a barber shop that had a sign, 'We buy gold,'" he says. "A barber shop! Can you imagine?"—AP /Kim Stegall

2011 gold rush

Amy Robinette owns Gold Buying Girl, a network of 70 women in six states who throw parties for people to sell their gold jewelry. She quit a career as a personnel recruiter to start the business two years ago. She says her clients "don't realize how much their gold is worth."

Sharlett Wilkinson Buckner, of Humble, Texas, recently took an old bracelet, ring and necklace to her local jeweler and walked out with $1,070.

"I couldn't wait for my husband to come home," she said. "I fanned my money in front of him and said, 'Look what I got for my gold.'"

The next day, he sold an old gold necklace for $650 .

"Once they sell, it kind of creates a frenzy," says Robinette. "They either want to find more or tell their friends and their friends start selling."

Above: Diamond-and-gold contact lenses adorn an Indian bride's eyes. She sees through the centers.

CWJ

After reading these two feature articles, make a list of the ways that they differ from short, informative news stories.

◄ IN YOUR JOURNAL

CAPSULE 2

1.4.2

PREPARING TO WRITE

WORLD WISDOM:

In your last CWJ entry, you noted elements of feature articles that make them different from regular news stories. Here's some advice from *WORLD* writer and news editor Jamie Dean:

Imagine opening a magazine and glancing at an article that started with this sentence: Many neighborhoods in Japanese cities are still covered in sludge from the tsunami that struck northeastern Japan last March.

Now imagine glancing at an article that began this way: In a sludge-covered neighborhood in northeastern Japan, a local church leader remembers the afternoon a tsunami destroyed his hometown and swallowed the house his family owned for three generations.

Which article would you continue reading? If you chose the second one, it's probably because you like reading interesting stories about real people. That's a good definition of a feature story. A feature story tells about current events through the perspective of someone living through the news.

When I traveled to Japan to report on recovery efforts six months after the tsunami struck, I met the church leader who lost his home. In my article, I wrote about the basic facts of his hometown, including how many people lost their homes, how many people died, and how much recovery work remained unfinished. But I told the church leader's story to show how the big picture affected one family living through hardship. Since it's easier to identify with people than statistics, readers appreciate learning about the lives of those affected by the news.

If you have an opportunity to write a feature story, keep those elements in mind. Try to find out as many facts as possible, but also try to find an interesting person who shows how the facts affect real life. Not only will your audience keep reading, they may even respond if there's a way to help the people you feature.

In the *Trak* features you read last time, did you note any of the elements Jamie Dean identifies as important to include in a feature article?

For the type of feature we're doing in this lesson, we don't want you to play on your readers' emotions, include your own opinions, or write several thousand words—though some features do. However, we DO want you to use more literary, interesting language ("stomach-churning volatility"), a "beginning, middle, end" structure, and transitions ("on the other hand, meanwhile"). These elements help keep your readers interested and move the story along.

In the last lesson, you should have chosen the topic you will write about in this lesson (see 1.3.4). Today, we want you to make all the preparations you need to begin writing in the next capsule. On your computer or on a separate sheet of paper, make two headings for yourself. Depending on your topic, you might want to name one list "Positives" or "Pros" and the other list "Negatives" or "Cons." If your controversy isn't a negative/positive dichotomy, you might want to label your two sides "Position 1" and "Position 2."

Now reread the articles you chose. As you read, make notes under each heading. Make sure to note WHERE you saw the information; write down the source. Your list might look something like this:

Negatives
▶ Cost of elite sports is high (St. James—"Costs typically run from $1,000 to $10,000 annually.")
▶ Kids are beginning to play at younger and younger ages. (St. James—"Some of the budding stars are as young as eight years old."
▶ A very small percentage of the kids get college scholarships. (Lynn O'Shaughnessy—"According to the NCAA, only 2 percent of high school athletes, roughly 130,000 kids, bag a full or partial scholarship.")

When you've finished with your first viewpoint, move on to your other viewpoint and do the same. Our recommendation is to quote the article EXACTLY in your notes. That way you can decide as you are writing your article if you want to quote your source or paraphrase it. It's important to know the exact words the author used so that you can either quote accurately or change the language sufficiently when you paraphrase.

When you have all relevant information from your written sources down on paper, read back through everything you've got so far. What questions do you have? Write them down, limiting yourself to 3 to 5 questions. Now look back at the potential sources you listed in 1.3.5. Which could best answer your questions? When you decide on the person you'd like to ask, you may need to tweak the questions a bit to fit that exact person.

Our final list of questions looked like this:
▶ How many years have you played club soccer?
▶ What is the name of your team?
▶ What were the positives of playing club soccer?
▶ What were the negatives of playing club soccer?
▶ Overall, are you glad you played or do you wish you hadn't?

Before interviewing, read back through capsules 1.2.3 and 1.2.4, following the directions once again to prepare for, schedule, and complete the interview.

Once you've finished the interview, transcribe it. Which side of your issue does the interview fit into? Negatives? Positives? A little of both? Add quotes from your interviewee to your lists.

Our new list of negatives would look like this:

Negatives
▶ Cost of elite sports is high (St. James 2—"Costs typically run from $1,000 to $10,000 annually.")
▶ Kids are beginning to play at younger and younger ages. (St. James 2—"Some of the budding stars are as young as eight years old."
▶ A very small percentage of the kids get college scholarships. (Lynn O'Shaughnessy—"According to the NCAA, only 2 percent of high school athletes, roughly 130,000 kids, bag a full or partial scholarship."
▶ **"It's a big time commitment and a big money commitment. I've seen it take a huge toll on some guys and their families." (Sawyer, Phone interview)**

When you think you're done, skim back over your stories and the transcription of the interview one more time. Did you leave any important information out? When you're satisfied that you're finished, move on to your CWJ.

CWJ

Today, using the lists you created, take some time thinking about how you will organize your story. Our suggestion would be:
▶ Find a quote, statistic, or an interesting strategy you will use to begin
▶ Viewpoint 1
▶ Viewpoint 2
▶ Quotation, statistic, or other information you will use to create a strong ending.

Another possible way to organize your story is alternating between pros and cons. However, we'd encourage you to make it easier for yourself by looking at one side as a whole and then the other.

How do you decide which to put first? Our interview helped us decide. Because the club soccer player we interviewed had a fairly positive experience with club sports, we decided to go with the negatives first and end with the personal perspective that included more positives. However, we could have done it either way. It's up to you.

When you think you know how you will organize your story, write down your organizational pattern in your CWJ.

◀ IN YOUR JOURNAL

WRITING ONE SIDE OF THE STORY

In this lesson, we'll be writing our feature along with you so that you have a model to work from. We're going to begin by writing an introduction and addressing one side of our topic—the negative side of elite or club sports for kids.

Having a Ball?

Some are up early each morning. Others are out late every night. They train hours each day and have a game or tournament nearly every weekend. We're not talking about professional athletes. We're talking about kids who play on year-round club or elite sports teams.

Some are as young as eight years old (St. James, "It's a Whole New Ballgame," WFAA, 16 May 2011). Before club teams began gaining popularity in the 1990s, the height of most kids' athletic experience was playing for their high school team. Today, by high school many kids have already burned out. When they begin playing year-round at age eight or nine, practicing several days a week, some get bored with the sport or no longer find it enjoyable.

Additionally, it can be expensive. To join a year-round club costs somewhere between a few hundred to a few thousand dollars annually. On top of that, families pay for uniforms, special shoes, balls, and other equipment. With frequent tournaments, families' out-of-pockets expenses can be even higher. Some teams travel across the country once a year or more to participate in tournaments. Team sports can be fun, but is it worth $1,000 to $10,000 annually (St. James)?

Parents are lured into signing their kids up by their belief—often encouraged by select team coaches—that their kid is "special." And what parent doesn't want to believe that their eight-year-old is the next Michael Jordan or Josh Hamilton? Many believe that putting a few thousand dollars a year into their preteen children's sports development is the ticket to a sports scholarship to college—and maybe even a professional career. The reality is, very few kids go to college on a sports scholarship: According to the NCAA, less than two percent get a full-ride scholarship to a Division I school. And of those, only a tiny fraction—one percent or less—go on to play professionally (O'Shaughnessy, "Playing for a Scholarship," CBS News 2 June 2009).

If kids begin playing one sport year-round at an early age, they increase their risk of repetitive motion or overuse injuries—injuries that result from using the same muscle groups exclusively. In his book, *Revolution in the Bleachers*, Regan McMahon says that some young pitchers may be ruining their chances to ever play professionally. Professional teams have begun to realize that pitchers only have so many throws before their arms are worn out. Too much play in childhood makes pitchers a bad risk for pro teams.

CWJ

Today, choose either the negative or the positive side of your controversy and write at least three to five paragraphs, using the lists you created and the organization you laid out in your CWJ in the last capsule.

Don't forget that you need an introduction that grabs attention. You might choose to begin with an interesting quote, a startling statistic, or as we did, a little bit of a mystery as to exactly what you are talking about.

When working with sources, make sure to cite them. When citing an article in an article, in parenthesis, cite the author's name, the name of the article, the news organization that it came from, and the date.

If you include a book, as we do, give the book's title and the author's name. If you quote an article more than once, after the first time, just cite the author's last name.

Note that we didn't cite every single sentence that we used. That's because much of what we included is general information that we saw in multiple sources. You don't need to cite general information.

◀ IN YOUR JOURNAL

CAPSULE 4   1.4.4

ANOTHER SIDE OF THE STORY

You're making great progress—you've already written about half of your feature article! Today, you'll write about the opposing view. Keep your lists and CWJ with your organizational plan handy.

Remember that strong verb choices and descriptive nouns and adjectives help to keep a longer piece like this one engaging for the reader. So use your best vocabulary!

We'll pick up where we left off with our feature:

> But when kids don't specialize in one sport too early and they don't over train, playing elite sports offers kids many benefits. According to the American Academy of Pediatrics, children who play sports are more fit and healthy than kids who do not. In "Intensive Training and Sports Specialization in Young Athletes," pediatricians on the Committee on Sports Medicine and Fitness discovered most children who play elite sports found it to be a positive experience.

Seventeen-year-old Sawyer Martin of Asheville, North Carolina, has played soccer for Highland Football Club since he was 13 years old. Soccer season is busy, with three to four mandatory practices per week as well as a game or a tournament each weekend. These away games often require travel and a hotel stay. During the off-season, there is one mandatory and two optional practices per week.

There are some negatives to devoting so much time to a sport such as missing other activities and social opportunities. But for Sawyer, the good outweighs the bad. He's learned the value of working hard—drilling a skill over and over for many years. "You gradually see yourself get better and better. Even though maybe it's only a little bit each week, eventually you master it," says Sawyer. He believes this mastery he's learned in soccer carries over into other areas of his life. "Soccer has given me the ability to stick with things."

Another perk is the friendships that Sawyer has formed with other players over the years. "We're really, really good friends. Because of soccer, we see each other a lot," he says.

"I've gained the ability to lead and to follow," says Sawyer. "When you're watching someone lead you think you could do a lot better. But when you get in that position, it's hard, but you figure it out. That's one of the biggest lessons people who play club soccer learn."

Sawyer is quick to say that club soccer isn't for everyone. "It's a big time commitment and a big money commitment. I've seen it take a huge toll on some guys and their families."

This past weekend, Sawyer, a senior in high school, played his last club soccer game. Looking back over his experience, though there are some things he would have changed, overall he thinks the commitment to his team has been worth it. "Soccer is a game I really love to play, and club soccer allowed me to play at a very high level," says Sawyer. "All in all, I came out of club soccer a better soccer player and a better person, as well."

CWJ

IN YOUR JOURNAL ▶

You've got a draft of your article! Take a break of at least a few hours. Then come back and read through the whole thing aloud, recording as you read. Next, play back the recording, listening specifically for any spots that are confusing and hard to understand. Does the article seem biased to one position or the other? Or do you believe you've been fair to both sides?

Make any changes you think are necessary.

CAPSULE 5

REVISING AND POLISHING

If you drafted on the computer, print out a clean copy of your feature article. You've had a substantial break since the last time you read through it. Today, we want you to work on strengthening your language as well as correcting the grammar issues we've been working on in this unit.

First, go through and circle all your verbs. Anywhere you see an "is, am, are, was, were, be, being, been," consider whether you can change the verb to a stronger one. Once you've done that, look at your other verbs. Are there any you can strengthen?

We saw two in our first two sentences:
Some are up early each morning. Others are out late every night.

We changed to:
Some rise early each morning. Others stay up late every night.

Go back through and underline all the nouns and pronouns. Do you see any that you could improve?

Here's one we saw that needed improvement:
Additionally, it can be expensive.

We changed to:
Additionally elite sports' teams can break the bank if families aren't careful.

Now that you have the nouns underlined and the verbs circled, check agreement. If you're having trouble, flip back to 1.3.5 to refresh your memory on how to make nouns and verbs agree. Remember, agreement sounds easy but has some tricky moments that can trip up great writers.

Next, circle all the commas. When you've done that, read aloud up to each comma and stop, checking to make sure it's a complete thought. (One big clue: Is there an underlined noun and a circled verb before the comma? If not, you probably don't have a complete thought.) Flip back to 1.1.1 for examples of ways to fix comma splices.

Finally, go through and check your quotes. Is all of your punctuation (commas, question marks, exclamation marks) inside the quotation marks? See 1.2.5 for a reminder. While you're checking for correct punctuation, check for accuracy as well. Check each quote in your feature article against the lists you made. Are the words identical? Did you leave anything out or change any words? Check to make sure you've included accurate source information in your citations as well.

When you've made the changes, print or write out a clean copy and give it to your parent/teacher. Ask her to use colored pencils and make the following notations:

1. RED—Underline a particularly well-written sentence.
2. ORANGE—Underline strong word choices (strong verbs, descriptive nouns)
3. BLUE—Underline any sections you find confusing. In the margin, write questions or comments to help the writer understand why you are confused.
4. LIGHT BLUE—Use this or another bright color to mark any grammar errors. If there are many, focus primarily on those covered in this unit (comma splices, subject-verb agreement, and punctuation with quotations).

At the end, the educator should write a note to the feature writer that answers these questions:
1. What do you think the writer has done particularly well in his or her feature article?
2. What one change do you believe would make the feature article stronger?
3. Does the article seem biased to one position or the other? Note a change or two the writer could make to create a more balanced article.

Once you get the comments, make a final revision that includes the changes your parent/teacher suggested.

Here's our revised article:

Having a Ball?

Some rise early each morning. Others stay up late every night. They train hours each day, and have a game or tournament nearly every weekend. We're not talking about professional athletes. We're talking about kids who play on year-round club or elite sports teams.

Some club players begin playing elite sports at eight years old (St. James, "It's a Whole New Ballgame," WFAA, 16 May 2011). Before club teams began gaining popularity in the 1990s, the height of most kids' athletic experience was playing for a high school team. Today, by high school many kids have already burned out. When children begin playing year-round at age eight or nine, practicing several days a week, some get bored with the sport or no longer find it enjoyable.

Additionally elite sports' teams can break the bank if families aren't careful.

The cost of joining a select team ranges from a few hundred to a few thousand dollars. On top of that, families pay for uniforms, special shoes, balls and other equipment. With frequent tournaments, families' out-of-pocket expenses can be even higher. Some teams travel across the country once a year or more to participate in tournaments. Team sports can be fun, but is it worth $1,000 to $10,000 annually (St. James)?

Parents are lured into signing their kids up by their belief—often encouraged by select team coaches—that their kid is "special." And what parent doesn't want to believe that their eight-year-old is the next Michael Jordan or Josh Hamilton? Many think that putting a few thousand dollars a year into their preteen child's sports development is his ticket to college—and maybe even a professional career. The reality is, very few kids go to college on a sports scholarship. According to the NCAA, less than two percent get a full-ride scholarship to a Division I school (O'Shaughnessy, "Playing for a Scholarship," CBS News 2 June 2009). And of those, only a tiny fraction—one percent or less—go on to play professionally.

If kids begin playing one sport year-round at an early age, they increase the risk of repetitive motion or overuse injuries—injuries that result from using the same muscle groups exclusively. In his book, Revolution in the Bleachers, Regan McMahon says that some young pitchers may be ruining their chances to ever play professionally. Professional teams have begun to realize that pitchers only have so many throws before their arms wear out. Too much play in childhood makes pitchers a bad risk for pro teams.

But when kids don't specialize in one sport too early and they don't over train, playing elite sports offers kids many benefits. According to the American Academy of Pediatrics, children who play sports are more fit and healthy than kids who do not. In "Intensive Training and Sports Specialization in Young Athletes," pediatricians determined most children who play elite sports find the experience positive.

Seventeen-year-old Sawyer Martin of Asheville, North Carolina, began playing soccer for Highland Football Club when he was 13 years old. During soccer season, Sawyer attends three to four mandatory practices per week. Weekends are filled with games and tournaments often requiring travel and a hotel stay. During the off-season, the Highland Football club holds one mandatory and two optional practices per week.

Negatives of devoting so much time to a sport include missing other activities and social opportunities. However, Sawyer says that the good outweighs the bad.

He's learned the value of working hard by drilling a skill over and over for many years. "You gradually see yourself get better and better. Even though maybe it's only a little bit each week, eventually you master it," says Sawyer. He believes this mastery he's learned in soccer carries over into other areas of his life. "Soccer has given me the ability to stick with things."

Another perk is the friendships that Sawyer has formed with other players over the years. "We're really, really good friends. Because of soccer, we see each other a lot," he says.

"I've gained the ability to lead and to follow," says Sawyer. "When you're watching someone lead you think you could do a lot better. But when you get in that position, it's hard, but you figure it out. That's one of the biggest lessons people who play club soccer learn."

Sawyer is quick to say that club soccer isn't for everyone. "It's a big time commitment and a big money commitment. I've seen it take a huge toll on some guys and their families."

This past weekend, Sawyer, a senior in high school, played his last club soccer game. Looking back over his experience, though there are some things he would have changed, overall he thinks the commitment to his team has been worth it. "Soccer is a game I really love to play, and club soccer allowed me to play at a very high level," says Sawyer. "All in all, I came out of club soccer a better soccer player and a better person, as well."

THE RIGHT WORD

Using the list of words provided, fill in the blank with the best word:

diverted	jot	refine
frenzy	libeled	salient
incontrovertible	notoriety	subsequent
incorporate	objective	succinct
jargon	paraphrase	transcribe

1. Journalistic style is more brief or _____ than most other writing styles.

2. A reporter should be _____, not biased.

3. The specialized language of a trade or profession is called _____.

4. Before you can use information from a recorded interview you must _____ it.

5. Writers _____ material from interviews into news stories.

6. In _____ quotes, you just need to identify the person being quoted by last name (and title if they have one)

7. Sometimes it's best to _____ a source.

8. Often a topic is controversial because there is no _____ evidence that supports one side or the other.

9. The media _____ surrounding Richard Jewell made many people rush to judgment, assuming he had committed the crime.

10. The inverted pyramid allows readers to get the most _____ points of the story by reading the headline and the first paragraph or two.

11. Educators are protesting a government action that _____ $74 million in education funds to Kenya's military.

12. Bring paper so you can _____ down any questions.

13. Mr. Jewell eventually sued many of the media outlets who _____ him in their stories.

14. Jesse James achieved _____ as a bank robber and train robber.

15. Do they use any other terms for your topic that might help _____ your search?

Write with WORLD

UNIT 2/ LESSON 1

CRAFTING AN OPINION

READING TO UNDERSTAND, READING TO QUESTION

CAPSULE 1

2.1.1

WHAT DO YOU THINK?

In the previous unit, you examined more than one side of an issue. You considered others' opinions. Those experiences will help you begin developing an on-paper **persona** in Unit 2.

We think too many writing programs start in the wrong place. They try to turn you into researchers, piling up lots of information and then building it into arguments—like you're building a model airplane or putting together a bookshelf. In our opinion, the point of writing isn't merely accumulating information and pouring it into a certain format, it's getting what you think down on paper. And we want you to learn to do that in a way that's clear and lively and interesting so that someone else will want to read it—and maybe even write something in return. In short, we want your writing to become part of a conversation.

A writing conversation can help you take what you think about something—your opinion—and inspire you to become knowledgeable about that topic. A gut feeling you have can be transformed into an informed opinion. It's likely that as you read what others have to say about a topic, it will refine what you think. And that's good.

Some of you may be thinking, "Great! I have lots of opinions! This will be easy for me!" Getting ideas down on paper may be your strength. But don't worry if you are a less-opinionated type. You have a strength too. You probably already see both sides of an issue—that's what makes it hard to choose a side. You're probably already thinking a lot about the issues. That's a good place to begin.

We're glad that all personality types can make good writers. The differences that make you a more impulsive or a more measured, cautious type are going to help make up the "on paper" persona you develop. What makes you different from everyone else—your sense of humor, your vocabulary, your personal experiences, your likes and dislikes, and a whole host of other quirks—means that no one looks at the world exactly the way that you do. That's what makes your opinions worth reading.

IN YOUR JOURNAL ▶

CWJ

Quickly read through this list. Write "agree" or "disagree" or "No opinion" after each. Don't think too hard.

- ▶ Teens text too much.
- ▶ Macs are better than PCs.
- ▶ Nike makes the best running shoes.
- ▶ People under 16 shouldn't drink coffee.
- ▶ Homeschooling kids get the best education.
- ▶ All high school graduates should go to college.
- ▶ Video games are a waste of time.

Most of you probably had at least one "no opinion"—in that list there's probably at least one thing you know or care little about. But did you have mostly "no opinion"? If so, you probably don't like to make judgments on the spot—you like to think harder before coming to an opinion. If you found you had an opinion about everything, that tells you a little about yourself, too. You tend to rely on your gut feelings.

Knowing which type of person you are before going into this unit can be helpful. If you're more opinion-ated, you may need to work harder to "listen" to what other writers have to say. If you typically withhold opinions, you may need to push yourself to make a **decisive** statement regarding what you think.

CAPSULE 2   2.1.2

DON'T BE A BLANK SLATE!

The earth is round. Water freezes at 32 degrees. Apples grow on trees. These statements are facts. If you open your ears and eyes, though, you'll realize that many of the statements you hear each day are people's opinions. You hear things like, "Don't go to that new restaurant on 7th Street. The food is terrible!" or, "Our basketball team should have won. Those refs were playing favorites!"

Opinions can be tricky. They are often presented as facts. Especially when you're reading the newspaper or looking at material on the Internet, you can get fooled if you're not careful. If you see something in print that says "Pizza is a vegetable," does that make it true? Right now, the government counts the tomato paste on pizza as a vegetable. That allows it to stay in public school cafeterias around the nation. But just because a newspaper headline says that pizza is a vegetable doesn't make it true. Even if Congress rules that pizza is a vegetable doesn't make it a fact. Whether or not pizza should count as a vegetable is debatable.

The message of this capsule is, "Don't be a blank slate." Especially when ideas are well-written and presented as facts, we can get confused. If an authority like the local paper includes an opinion piece that sounds true, you might assume that it is. If you don't carefully question each idea to see if it's really a fact or rather an opinion dressed as a fact, you'll be like that blank slate. People can write their opinions on you. Instead of forming your own viewpoint, you become a parrot who simply repeats other people's ideas.

CWJ

Take a look at the following sentences. Put an F in front of facts and an O in front of opinions.

_____ The Phillies are a better baseball team than the Yankees.

_____ Smoking causes cancer.

_____ Regular brushing of teeth helps prevent cavities.

_____ Honey is the best natural sweetener.

_____ Of all animals, dogs make the best pets.

_____ Christmas is the most important holiday because it celebrates Christ's birth.

_____ Antarctica is the coldest place on earth.

_____ Starbucks sells more coffee than any other coffeehouse company, making it the best coffeehouse company in the world.

CAPSULE 3   2.1.3

"LISTENING" TO OTHER WRITERS' OPINIONS

WORLD WISDOM

We've just told you not to be a blank slate. However, before you begin questioning a piece of writing, you need to make sure you understand what the writer is saying. If you come to an article looking for a fight, you can easily miss the writer's point.

When you first read an article, we want you to focus on understanding what the writer is saying. In this World Wisdom, *God's World News* writer and editor Rebecca Cochrane provides some tips on reading to understand. We've bolded the section we want you to pay particular attention to:

Reading for me is always an interactive experience. But the subject matter determines the nature of the interaction.

If I'm reading a textbook or other scholarly work that requires intense concentration, I do so with a pen and notebook alongside. To make the knowledge my own, I rewrite key ideas in the notebook in my own words. This helps increase retention. If I can't explain an idea in my own words, I can't be sure I really grasped the knowledge at all.

A magazine or news article gets treated more casually, but there are always a few questions in the back of my mind while I read. Afterward, I review those questions to see if I really took in what the article was about. What is the main idea? Is the writer telling what happened, or is he trying to persuade me to reach a certain conclusion? Were all sides of the story considered? Do the details support the main idea or conclusion well?

A work of fiction gets completely different treatment. If it's a good story, then mentally, I enter into it. The setting and characters become such a part of my thinking while I'm absorbed in a good novel that I carry them with me into the rest of my day. For instance, when reading through the Chronicles of Narnia, *I'll find myself—in my imagination—narrating my own* **mundane** *daily chores in a British accent. I might imagine myself in a friendly "row" with Trumpkin over how best to fold the towels, or whether those particular socks actually make a match. Then returning to the book is like a reunion with old friends. I open the pages and we pick up right where we left off.*

Like Mrs. Cochrane, we've figured out that we must be active readers if we want to fully grasp what another writer is saying. Just letting our eyes glide over the words is not enough. Today, you'll be reading an article by Gene Edward Veith that appeared in the November 15, 2003 issue of *WORLD Magazine*. As you read, focus on understanding. We'll consider Dr. Veith's opinions and the questions they raise in the next capsule.

Brand Names
By Gene Veith

Names, the **emblems** of a person's identity, used to mean something. "Abraham" means "father of a multitude." "Moses" means "draws out," as of the River Nile and as he would draw the people out of slavery. "Jesus" means "God saves," so that His very name testifies to His deity and His saving work.

In tribal societies, people are sometimes named for animals ("Sitting Bull") or for something else in nature ("Red Cloud"). In the Middle Ages, children born on a Saint's Day were named for that saint, giving them their **patron** saint. Puritans started naming their children after virtues, such as Faith and Prudence, or after other abstractions such as Increase.

The main criterion for names today, though, is not so much their meaning as whether they sound good. Some parents, in order to ensure their child's utter individuality, make up unique names, a set of musical syllables and unusual spellings designed to ensure that no one else in the world has exactly that name.

Pop culture (the world of entertainment and commercialism) is driving out traditional culture. We see this in many areas, including education and the church. Now, it's showing up in the names people choose for their children. Decades from now, adults will find themselves saddled with the names of by then old-fashioned pop stars who happened to have been big at the time their mothers gave birth. Television characters also influence the names of real babies.

A new trend in baby names, however, takes the pop-culture influence to a new level. Cleveland Evans, a psychology professor at Nebraska's Bellevue University and a member of the American Name Society, studied Social Security records for the year 2000 and found that many children today are being named after consumer products.

Twenty-two girls registered in 2000 were named "Infiniti." Not "Infinity" with a "y," as in the illimitable attribute of God, but "Infiniti" with an "i," as in the car. There were also 55 boys named "Chevy" and five girls named "Celica."

Hundreds of children were named after clothing companies. There were 298 girls named "Armani." There were 164 named after the more casual "Nautica." Six boys were named "Timberland," after the boot.

Sometimes the clothing namesakes are more generic, with a special emphasis on fabrics. Five girls were named "Rayon." Six boys were named "Cashmere," seven were named "Denim," and five were named "Cotton" (though perhaps this was for Increase Mather's son).

Forty-nine boys were named "Canon," after the camera. Seven boys were named "Del Monte," apparently in honor of canned vegetables. Twenty-one girls were named "L'Oreal," after the hair dye, presumably to let them know that "you are worth it."

"Sky" might be the name of a nature-loving flower child's offspring, but 23 girls and 6 boys were named "Skyy." This is a brand of vodka. Parents are naming their children after other alcoholic beverages, too. Nine girls were named "Chianti." Six boys were named "Courvoisier."

Perhaps the ultimate product name for kids uncovered by Mr. Evans was ESPN. Two separate parents, one in Texas and one in Michigan, named their sons after the sports cable network. A reporter for the *Dallas Morning News* traced down the family of big sports fans and learned that the correct pronunciation of little ESPN's name is "espen."

So what does this mean? Are children being seen in the same terms as consumer products or other possessions? Certainly, just as there are trophy wives, there are now trophy children.

Certainly parents have the right to name a child anything they want. It is wrong to give someone a hard time just for having an unusual name.

For some, the "Christian name," as it is called, is given at baptism. The name's true significance comes from that one individual identity being identified with and joined to a greater name: "ESPN, I baptize you in the name of the Father, Son, and Holy Spirit."

Christians find their own name and identity—whatever it is—in the name of Jesus, "God saves."

CWJ

For your CWJ, you'll need a pen and paper, a highlighter, and a dictionary. Read through the article once. As you read, when you find a word you don't know the meaning of, circle it. When you finish, look up the meaning of the words and write out (or type) the definitions. You should also look up any references you don't understand. For instance, if you don't know what a trophy wife is, you should look it up on the Internet. We'll do this one for you to help you understand. We typed "what is a trophy wife" into the search engine Google. We were directed to this explanation on Wikipedia: "Trophy wife is an expression used to refer to a wife, usually young and attractive, who is regarded as a status symbol for the husband, who is often older and wealthy."

Now go back through again, underlining the key points. (Dr. Veith helped you out by using good topic sentences for his paragraphs.) Write (or type) a short summary of the article in your own words. Putting it in your own words will help you to better absorb and understand the ideas. Shoot for 12-20 sentences total (one or two sentences per paragraph).

When you've finished your summary, write or type one sentence that tells the main point of the article. When completed, add this page to your CWJ.

We'll get you started by summarizing the first two paragraphs:

Names are symbols for people; when they hear your name, they think of you. Names used to represent a person's character and personality; for instance "Jesus" means "God Saves."

Other ways of choosing names for people have included naming them after animals, nature, saints, and virtues.

QUESTIONING OTHER WRITERS' OPINIONS

Let's begin this capsule by looking back at your CWJ for capsule 2. Which sentences did you say were fact and which were opinion? Here are the correct answers:

_____ The Phillies are a better baseball team than the Yankees.

_____ Smoking causes cancer.

_____ Regular brushing of teeth helps prevent cavities.

_____ Honey is the best natural sweetener.

_____ Of all animals, dogs make the best pets.

_____ Christmas is the most important holiday because it celebrates Christ's birth.

_____ Antarctica is the coldest place on earth.

_____ Starbucks sells more coffee than any other coffeehouse company, making it the best coffeehouse company in the world.

Did you get the correct answers? Some opinions are easy to recognize. When a writer says something is "the best," that's usually an opinion. For one thing, what are your criteria for the best? When you're talking about honey, do you mean the healthiest? The sweetest? Does it work better than other natural sweeteners in cooking?

Sometimes, when an opinion is combined with a fact, it can be tricky. For instance, Starbucks sells the most coffee of all coffeehouse companies. But does that make it the best? It still depends on your criteria. Other coffeehouses might sell higher quality coffee or more flavorful coffee. If we changed "best coffee-house" to "most popular coffeehouse," this sentence would be a fact instead of an opinion.

As you can see, distinguishing fact from opinion takes careful, close reading—a small change in wording can change a fact into an opinion. In order to decide whether or not you agree with an opinion, you must first recognize it as an opinion.

CWJ

Today, we want you to reread "Brand Names." This time though, we want you to highlight any sentence you find that's an opinion. Write them on a separate sheet of paper. When you've done so, skim back over the article once more. What questions do those opinions raise for you? What other questions does the article make you ask? We want you to read skeptically—as a doubter. Write or type at least three questions. (Add them to the paper on which you wrote/typed the opinions in the article.) Add the sheet of paper to you CWJ.

◀ IN YOUR JOURNAL

We'll get you started: "The main criterion for names today, though, is not so much their meaning as whether they sound good." *Is this really true? I think I know more people who name their kids after family members than choose names just because they sound good.*

CAPSULE 5 2.1.5

READING TO JOIN THE CONVERSATION

Before reading "Brand Names," had you thought about babies' names and why people choose them? Probably not too much, right?

Did reading the article give you any new thoughts or ideas about names? Perhaps it even made you want to respond in some way or discuss names with someone. That's good. One of the most important reasons for the kind of reading we're teaching you to do in this lesson is to become part of a conversation. We want you to become interested in ideas. There's no better way to do so than to read other people's ideas and write about them or discuss them with others. That's what we mean by joining the conversation.

IN YOUR JOURNAL ▶

CWJ

Today in your CWJ, write your own ideas or opinions about names. Here are a couple of questions to get you started if you're having trouble:

1. What factors do you think parents should consider when they name their children?
2. Do you think the names people are given make a difference in the type of people they become?

STYLE TIME

Reading is essential for joining the conversation and exploring ideas. But it's just as important for your writing style. If you don't read, it's easy to get words that sound similar mixed up. The best way to learn how words are spelled and used is to read them in context.

In this Style Time, we're going to list a few common words people use incorrectly. We'd like for you to begin a new tab in your CWJ called "usage." Start a page called Wrong Words on your computer or on a piece of notebook paper. From now on, whenever you have a wrong word error in your writing, log it in the usage section of your CWJ. That way, before a paper is due, you can check them against this list. Sometimes we use wrong words because they sound almost the same as another word in speech. We'll look at a few examples of this type of wrong word in this lesson.

Than/Then

Than is usually used in comparisons: He owns a better bike than I do.
Then is a word indicating time: First I need to do my homework, then I can relax.

Accept/Except

Accept means to agree to take or to receive something: I accept your offer.
Except means excluding: Everyone was invited except me.

Affect/Effect

Affect means to influence something: Two weeks of rain affected our soccer schedule.
An *effect* is the result of something: The effect of the medicine was almost immediate.

Loose/Lose

Loose means not tight: The handle on the front door is loose.
Lose means not winning or to misplace or to no longer possess: Did you lose your soccer match?

Advice/Advise

Advice is a noun meaning someone's opinion: I would value your advice as I make this decision.
Advise is a verb meaning the act of giving advice: Please advise me on this important issue.

If any of these are problem words for you, add them to the "wrong word" section of your CWJ.

THE RIGHT WORD

 Below are the five vocabulary words in context for this week. You should already have defined them in your journal as you found them in the reading.

1. Those are good steps toward what we want you to begin doing in this unit—developing an on-paper **persona**.
2. If you typically withhold opinions, you may need to push yourself to make a **decisive** statement regarding what you think.
3. I'll find myself—in my imagination—narrating my own **mundane** daily chores in a British accent.
4. Names, the **emblems** of a person's identity, used to mean something.
5. In the Middle Ages, children born on a Saint's Day were named for that saint, giving them their **patron** saint.

Using your thesaurus, try to find the BEST word to replace the bold word in the sentence. If you aren't familiar with the meanings of all the synonyms for each word in the thesaurus, you may need to use your dictionary to look them up. That way you can choose the word that best fits the sentence.

Write with
WORLD

UNIT 2 / LESSON 2

CRAFTING AN OPINION

CRITIQUING AN OPINION

CAPSULE 1

2.2.1

FIGURING OUT WHY YOU DISAGREE

♪ Can you think of a time when you've read something that **rankled** you? You knew you didn't agree with the writer, but you weren't exactly sure why. In this lesson, we're going to show you some ways that you can figure it out. If you can't **articulate** what it is you disagree with in someone's writing, you can't have a conversation. It's likely your discussion will collapse into name-calling and rapidly move away from the issue. This isn't edifying for either the writer or the reader. The goal of conversation on an issue—whether written or spoken—should be to seek truth.

So how do you figure out exactly why you disagree with a writer? In this lesson, we'll teach you to look for basic elements any opinion piece should contain. Once you can break down an opinion piece in this way, you can see more clearly where and why you disagree with a writer.

CWJ

Today, we'll look at another opinion editorial piece from the April 25, 2009 issue of *WORLD Magazine*. (We've shortened and simplified it a bit.) As you did with "Brand Names" in the last unit, read first to understand. If you're unsure of the meaning of any of the words, look them up. When you've finished reading, write a brief summary of the article in your own words.

Something Missing
Janie B. Cheaney

Few words were spoken more during the 9/11 crisis than "hero." It was applied to firefighters, police, and anyone who showed up to give blood. It was as if thinking heroically would make us heroic, even if all we did was gather at dusk and light candles. When the hysteria died down so did the **hyperbole**, for the most part.

But the idea of the ideal hero doesn't go away. It's been a fixture of literature and storytelling since time began. In ancient literature, "heroic" usually meant strong and fearless. That's pretty much it. Achilles' pride did not disqualify him, nor did Odysseus' deception.

The Mighty Men of David's time were acclaimed mostly for their body count. There were monsters on the loose, and only fearless strength could defeat them. Aristotle added complexity with his definition of "tragic hero": a noble figure brought down by his own fatal flaw. However, the tragic hero often regained stature through suffering.

We no longer believe in the fearless strength of heroes. We've created the ironic category of "superhero," which we only use for fictional characters. Aristotle's hero with all his flaws is no longer considered a hero at all but rather an "anti-hero." Today, a plain old hero can be anybody we look up to, whether in the highest positions of authority or around the kitchen table. That's fine—far better to look up to somebody than down on everybody.

The latest Harris poll on the subject of heroes contains both good news and bad. In answer to the question, "Who do you admire enough to call a hero?" Barak Obama's name came up more often than Jesus's name. This is not as ominous as it might appear. Respondents could name up to three individuals, and they were not given a list to choose from. So it's heartening that Jesus, who was not being inaugurated that month and has not dominated news cycles for the last two years, still came in second.

Perhaps more interesting, though, is agreement on what makes a hero. In the poll, participants were offered a list of qualities. They were asked if each figured to a large degree, a lesser degree, or none at all in their definition of a hero. "Doing what's right regardless of personal consequences" came in first, followed by "Not giving up until the goal is accomplished." These are definitions of courage and determination. Both are noble qualities, but something is missing in this definition of "hero."

What happened to the idea of self-sacrifice? The closest to that on the survey was "Willingness to risk personal safety to help others," and it polled sixth, after "Staying level-headed in a crisis." Yet self-sacrifice is what made our eyes well up at the news of firefighters rushing into the World Trade Center, knowing they might never come out.

Self-sacrifice is a major qualification for the Purple Heart, often awarded after death because the recipient has made the ultimate sacrifice. It is the path of heroism blazed by the One who emptied Himself and lay down His life for His sheep—an example that has haunted the Western world ever since. Other attributes mentioned in the survey contribute to heroism. However the attribute that actually **constitutes** it, to many minds, didn't come up.

So while it's nice that Jesus came in second, the reason is unclear. Because He "overcame adversity"? "Did more than what was expected of Him"? These are self-advancing qualities, not self-denying ones—and that may say something about what has quietly stolen out of our culture.

When the question "Who do you admire enough to call a hero?" was first asked in a 2001 Harris survey, 96 percent responded with at least one hero. In January, only 68 percent did. The remaining 32 percent either had no heroes or couldn't think of any. The cynicism that has infected the media may play a part in that. But if we've lost sight of the major component of heroism, is it any wonder that we begin losing sight of heroes?

CAPSULE 2

2.2.2

DO I AGREE WITH THE WRITER'S WORLDVIEW?

In *Write with WORLD I*, we talked about worldviews. To refresh your memory, a person's worldview is the beliefs that determine how he looks at the world and lives his life. Everyone has a worldview. And in 1.3.2 of this book, we showed you that even when a writer is trying to be unbiased, his worldview often shows up somewhere in the story. The picture they choose, the quotations they include, or even the topic of the story itself can reveal the writer's worldview.

In a piece like this one by Mrs. Cheaney, a major purpose of the article is for the writer to share her opinion. That's why it's called an opinion editorial. When a writer reveals her opinions, it often makes finding her worldview very easy. It's usually right there on the page.

When you begin breaking down an article to determine where exactly you agree with and disagree with a writer, the first question you should ask is "What's the writer's worldview?" For if you fundamentally disagree with the writer in the way you look at the world, you will probably disagree with her on at least some points in the essay.

Let's look at an example. Perhaps your family has a great love for animals. As Christians, you understand the dominion that God gave man over animals (Genesis 1:26) to be a great responsibility. You believe animals should be treated with kindness and respect, even when they are used for food or labor—both of which the Bible clearly allows. Let's imagine you read an article on animal cruelty. You agree with nearly every point that the writer makes about how animals should be treated. However, because the article's author doesn't believe in God, you don't agree with the *why* behind her argument—her worldview. She believes that animal life is just as valuable as human life, a belief that goes against your worldview. So while you may agree with a writer's points, you may disagree with her worldview.

In today's CWJ, we want you to read through Mrs. Cheaney's essay once again and ask some questions to help determine her worldview.

CWJ

Read through "Something Missing" again and answer the following questions:

1. What does the article reveal about the writer's worldview?
2. Who or what does she look to as an authority? (The Bible? Science? Her own feelings?)

CAPSULE 3   2.2.3

DO I AGREE WITH THE WRITER'S DEFINITIONS?

Definitions are another important foundation in an argument. If you don't agree with the writer's definitions, that's going to affect your assessment of the argument's validity. For instance, say you were reading an article about a Christian's duty to show love. In the article, the writer defines a Christian as "anyone who shares the love of Christ with the world around them." Then he goes on to say, "Some people may call the source of this love Buddha or Allah, or they may not call it anything at all. The important thing is that the love be shared."

By zeroing in on this definition, you can quickly see that it doesn't measure up to the biblical definition of a Christian. Focus on a writer's definitions (if he includes any). Determining whether or not you agree with them can help you to break down an argument and figure out how your opinion differs from the writer's.

Sometimes, though, the definition is debatable. In cases like these, you might partially or even mostly agree with the writer. Even so, you might still have a small quibble with it—maybe you think the writer should slightly change or add to her definition to make it clearer or more precise.

For example, let's look at the definition of a hero. The main point of "Something Missing," is that the definition no longer means what it used to for many Americans—it's been reduced to "doing what's right" and "not giving up." In Mrs. Cheaney's opinion, these characteristics alone are not enough. Self-sacrifice is what makes a hero a hero.

But her opinion may be in the minority. The Merriam-Webster Dictionary Online includes four possible meanings for the word "hero." None include the idea of self-sacrifice.

Unlike the first example, which is a clear-cut wrong definition, a definition that is debatable may take more time to figure out. Sometimes you'll find that a definition doesn't exactly seem wrong but for some reason doesn't seem quite right either. In cases like these, it may take some deep thought on your part to figure out why.

CWJ

In today's CWJ, we want you to come up with your own definition of a hero. That way, you'll be able to compare your definition to Mrs. Cheaney's and see whether the definitions differ.

1. Begin by listing three people—real or historical—that you believe are heroes:

    Like this:
    My Dad   Abraham Lincoln   Jesus Christ

2. Under each, list the qualities that you think made or make them heroic.

3. Compare the lists. What qualities are common to all three? Is there one or more that seem to be essential?

4. Finish by writing a one-sentence definition of a hero.

5. Did your definition differ from Mrs. Cheaney's or add to it in some way? Explain.

◀ IN YOUR JOURNAL

CAPSULE 4
2.2.4

IS THE ARGUMENT LOGICAL?

So if you agree with a writer's worldview and definitions, the argument must be good, right? Not necessarily. If something still doesn't add up, the next thing to check is the argument itself. Is it logical?

We could get into all sorts of word formulas here: "All men are mortal. I am a man. Therefore, I am mortal." This is formal logic. Certainly studying reasoning helps you identify logic in writing. We recommend it. But you can determine whether or not an argument is logical without taking a whole course on it.

The first thing you need to examine is the author's main claim. (A claim is simply the statement the writer's argument is based on.) Often the claim comes right up front in the first paragraph or two. However, in Op Ed pieces like "Something Missing," it can be found almost anywhere. In this case, Mrs. Cheaney builds toward her claim and doesn't get to it until paragraph six, more than halfway through the essay.

Cover up the next paragraph. Can you find her claim? If you need a hint, look at the essay's title.
If you chose the paragraph's final sentence, you are correct: "Both are noble qualities, but something

is missing in this definition of 'hero.'" How do you know this is the central claim? Because everything before that point is background. It's mostly factual. That sentence is the point where she first offers her own opinion of what makes a hero a hero. Everything after makes a case for what she believes is missing—self-sacrifice.

Once you've located the claim, you need to evaluate it. Does it make sense? Do you agree with it? If you disagree with the main point the writer is arguing, you probably won't agree with much that he or she is saying. For instance, if you think being fearless is the essential characteristic of a hero, you will disagree with Mrs. Cheaney's main claim. If so, you've figured out where you disagree.

But what if you are at least willing to consider the claim? Having a believable claim is a good start. The next question to ask is, "How well has the writer supported that claim? What evidence does she provide?" In the case of "Something Missing," Mrs. Cheaney uses examples to support her claim. She talks about the firefighters who rushed into the World Trade Center, knowing they might never come out on 9/11. She points to the Purple Heart, an award given by the military for bravery, often after death. Christ's death is her central example of self-sacrifice.

From these she draws her conclusion: "if we've lost sight of the major component of heroism, is it any wonder that we begin losing sight of heroes?"

Do her examples serve as strong evidence for her case? We believe it does. This essay was written for *WORLD Magazine*. Most readers are Christians who support the military and believe that Christ's sacrifice is the single most important event in history. If the readership were a group of atheists, this evidence would not be convincing. However, in this instance, it works well.

In general then, determining if an argument is logical involves 1) finding the author's claim and evaluating it, and 2) examining the evidence for the claim and determining whether it supports the claim and leads to the author's conclusion.

There are many other logical traps that an argument can fall into that blow it off course and ruin its logic. These traps are called **fallacies**. In general, they are specific ways that evidence can fail to support the claim. If you focus on making sure the evidence sticks to proving the claim (and doesn't shift in the middle to attacking another author or making a different argument completely), you're well on your way to being able to recognize a logical argument.

CWJ

IN YOUR JOURNAL ▶

Compare these two claims and their evidence, then explain which you think is more logical and why.

1. The legal age to drive should be raised to 18.
   ▶ With greater age comes wisdom.

- ▶ In two years, cars will have more safety features.
- ▶ Students would benefit from taking driver's education.

2. The legal age to drive should remain 16.
   - ▶ At 16, most students have at least two years to gain experience as drivers with parental supervision before they leave home for college.
   - ▶ Many 16-year-olds have jobs, and they need to drive to get to work.
   - ▶ Responsible teens should not be limited because a few 16-year-olds are not mature enough to drive safely. Parents of irresponsible teens should make the decision to keep them off the road; this shouldn't be imposed by the government.

CAPSULE 5
2.2.5

DO YOU *REALLY* DISAGREE?

Today, we want you to reflect a little on disagreement. Sometimes we form an opinion that is wrong. This World Wisdom by *Trak* writer and editor Kim Stegall demonstrates that we need to make sure that we are open to other opinions, even opinions that are critical of your ideas. If you're willing to listen to another opinion, you might just find out that you agree.

WORLD WISDOM

One of the most humbling critiques I ever received was from the editor of my first children's picture book. I had pored over that 36-page, 997-word book for months. I thought I had the perfect buildup of tension in my story about a young African boy who meets a lion in the forest: I described the sweat streaming down the boy's back and the cramping of his leg muscles after an all-night standoff with the beast. I could almost feel perspiration on my own palms. Kids will love this, I thought.

My editor wasn't impressed. She said, "Time means nothing to children. Five minutes is the same as five hours or five days. You're gonna have to rewrite this whole middle part. Make it exciting."

What?!? Didn't she know how hard I'd worked on that thrilling, nail-biting passage? It was somewhat sickening. And annoying. Not to mention embarrassing.

I told my husband what my editor had said. "Don't change it," he said. "It's right just the way it is."

I didn't think I could rework the story. But I decided to try.

"Don't change it," said my husband.

I changed it. I added dwarf mongooses, giant black bats, a deadly snake, a green frog, and a yellow-billed hornbill. That boy had quite a night before encountering the lion.

I read over what I'd done. It seemed good. It seemed scarier than cramps and sweat.

I gave the new pages to my husband. He was quiet. "What?" I asked.

"It's better," he said. "Way better."

My editor was right. I learned that editors and others who give input to writers often have valuable insights that a writer can't always see without help. Swallowing pride and listening to constructive criticism is a skill everyone—not just writers—can benefit from.

CWJ

IN YOUR JOURNAL ▶

Can you think of a time when you changed your opinion? What caused the change? Write a short paragraph about this experience.

STYLE TIME

In the last Style Time we examined one reason people use wrong words: they're spelled in a similar way or they sound similar when spoken. Today we'll look at some words people often use improperly. Once again, we want you to begin keeping track of these usage errors and others like them in your writing. Log your usage mistakes under the "wrong word" tab in your CWJ. Then you can check your writing against this list of mistakes you commonly make before turning in an assignment.

Farther/Further
Farther relates to physical distance—think of it as "more far": I can throw the ball *farther* than you can. Use *further* when the distance is not literal: Nothing could be *further* from the truth. ("The truth" can't be found in a specific place, so we use further.) *Further* also means "to advance": I intend to *further* my education by attending college.

Lie/Lay
This one is pretty easy in the present tense:
Lie has no direct object. It means "to recline": She went to *lie* down.
Lay must have a direct object. It means "to put or place something."
I like to remember this one by thinking of the first line of the well-known bedtime prayer: Now I *lay* me down to sleep. It's an awkward construction (and actually *lay* myself down would be more correct), but "me" serves as a direct object. You must have one with *lay*. Use this prayer to help you remember

You can't *lay* down in the present tense, you must have an object—a brush, a hat, a towel, or in this case "me"—to lay.

It gets trickier once you get past the present tense: *lay* is the past tense of lie. That's probably why people get mixed up. Copy this chart into the "wrong word" section of your journal. If you use *lie* or *lay*, check usage against this chart:

Present Tense	Past Tense	Past Participle
lie, lying	lay	have, has, had lain
lay, laying	laid	have, has, had laid

Gone/Went
We could give you a bunch of detailed grammatical information about why and when you use *gone* and *went*. However, this is a pretty easy fix, so we're just going to tell you how to fix the problem. *Gone* always needs a helping verb (such as is, has, have, has been); *went* never needs one.
So you may either say: He *has gone* to the store or He *went* to the store, but you would NEVER say, He *gone* to the store, or He *has went* to the store. Got it?

Bring/Take
Bring means movement TOWARD the speaker; *take* means movement AWAY from the speaker. So imagine you are sitting on chair. You could say, "Mom, can you *bring* me a snack?" or you could say to your little brother, "Percy, will you *take* this plate to the kitchen for me?" If he's sitting next to you, he would say, "*Take* it yourself!" but if he's in the kitchen he would say "*Bring* it yourself!" It all depends on location.

Supposeably, Supposedly
We saved the easiest one for last. There's never a reason to use the word *supposeably*. Though technically a word meaning "able to be supposed," we've never heard it used properly in speech or writing. Use the word *supposedly*. This means "generally assumed or believed." Usually when someone uses the word *supposedly*, they are casting doubt upon that belief or assumption: She supposedly practices an hour a day, but she never seems to get any better at playing the piano.

THE RIGHT WORD

Below are the five vocabulary words in context for this week. You should already have defined them in your journal as you found them in the reading.

1. Can you think of a time when you've read something that **rankled** you?
2. If you can't **articulate** what it is you disagree with in someone's writing, you can't have a conversation.
3. When the hysteria died down so did the **hyperbole**, for the most part.

4. However the attribute that actually **constitutes** it, to many minds, didn't come up.
5. These traps are called **fallacies**.

Using your thesaurus, try to find the BEST word to replace the bold word in the sentence. If you aren't familiar with the meanings of all the synonyms for each word in the thesaurus, you may need to use your dictionary to look them up. That way you can choose the word that best fits the sentence.

Write with WORLD

CAPSULE 1   2.3.1

HOW DO I RESPOND?

 You need a new coat. You're shopping with your mother. She helpfully holds up a blue hooded parka. "I like this one," she says.

"That's ugly! And I hate the color blue!" you shout at your mother. You hold up a green pea coat. "Buy me this one, instead!" What are the chances your mother is going to honor that "request"? With that ungrateful attitude, you may go home empty-handed!

Over the next two lessons, we're going to learn how to respond to an opinion you don't agree with. If you're not careful, *how* you respond—your tone—can completely **obscure** your message. Your reader will be paying more attention to your nasty attitude than what you're trying to say.

Just as important, we want you to learn to look for places in an argument where you and a person with an opposing viewpoint can agree. In this case, you and your mother agree that you need a new coat. By beginning from this shared opinion, the two of you can work to find other shared opinions. What colors do both of you like? What styles do both of you think suit you? How warm does the coat need to be? You may never fully agree on a favorite coat, but by looking for points where you can agree, you can at least have a productive discussion.

As in the last two lessons, we want you to begin by reading an essay. This one is written by fictional Professor Ross E. Frop. (We wanted to provide a controversial essay for you to disagree with, so we invented Professor Frop for this purpose.) Today, read the essay to understand. Don't get caught up in disagreeing with his ideas or being offended by his tone. Just make sure you clearly understand his claim and reasons.

Stix? Stone? Names can Hurt!

Apple? Peaches Honeyblossom? Diva Muffin? These are actual names Americans have given their children. You have to wonder if these parents thought they were ordering lunch instead of choosing the name that would go on their child's birth certificate!

When I was naming my children (with a little help from my wife, of course), I chose good, solid names that would be assets to my children. I didn't want them to stand out like a sore thumb or be the class joke. James Alexander and Margaret Anne—these are names that roll off the tongue and will serve them well as children and adults. Everyone should take naming their children as seriously as I did. And just in case they don't, we should follow the lead of countries like Denmark and France that strictly regulate the naming of children.

Denmark has a list of about 7,000 preapproved names, some for boys, others for girls. If you want to give your child a name that's not found on the list, you must get permission from your local church. The church sends it on to government officials. These officials review the name and decide whether or not it's acceptable. If not, parents must submit another name.

The law also protects children from being given a surname as a first name. This practice—which Americans have gone wild about in the last 30 years or so—is frankly ridiculous. When the practice first began, I'd hear a parent call out, "Grayson!" or "Jenner!" and look around for their butler. Who names a child something that makes them sound like a British servant? What are these parents thinking?

Perhaps worse yet, parents have begun naming their children after products. Sure, it's much cheaper to name a baby "Bentley" than to buy one of these cars. (They start at $189,000). However, do you really want your child to have to spend the first five minutes explaining why their parents named them L'Oreal or Del Monte every time they meet someone? And just think of what these absurd monikers do to children once they hit the job market. Be honest. Which job applicant's resume are you going to take more seriously—Moxie CrimeFighter's or Margaret Anne's?

Another reason we should institute stricter baby-naming laws is to eliminate gender confusion. (If men would keep their hair cut short that would help too, but that's a subject for another essay.) I don't want to have to guess whether someone is male or female; his or her name should tell me. But here in America, when I get my class roll, it's full of Taylors, Sawyers, and Rileys—names that parents apparently feel suit both genders. We need to follow the lead of countries like Germany and Denmark, where names are strictly divided into separate categories by gender.

Gender-specific names would also eliminate another problem I find particularly **nettling**: the **appropriation** of male names for female use. To begin with, there are fewer male names than female names—we can't afford to lose any. And yet parents steal from the male list, their own selfish desires outweighing the damage they do. Who will apologize to the male Ashleys, Leslies, Carols, Kellys, Tracys, and Stacys—all perfectly legitimate boy names before some thoughtless parents decided they would be cute girl names?

We need to stop the senseless practice of allowing parents carte blanche in naming their babies. Clearly, many parents unthinkingly bestow names that will at best merely cause their child ridicule in school and at worst cripple them professionally as adults.

I'm going out on a limb here, but I would go so far as to argue that better naming laws might make us better people. Wouldn't you find it easier to be dignified and proper if your name were James Alexander rather than Pilot Inspektor?

CWJ

Read through the essay once. As you read, circle a word if you don't know its meaning. Underline the key points. When you finish, look up the meaning of the words you circled. Next, write (or type) a short summary of the article in your own words (about one or two sentences per paragraph) and add it to your CWJ.

◀ IN YOUR JOURNAL

CAPSULE 2   2.3.2

UNTANGLING ARGUMENT AND TONE

As you read Professor Frop's essay, did you find it hard to summarize without adding in your opinions? We designed the professor to be a bit **sanctimonious** and condescending. Since he acts like his opinion should be law and that he's smarter than his readers, it's tempting to attack him personally rather than focusing on the points he makes in his argument.

We don't particularly like his *tone*. By tone we mean his attitude toward his readers and the material he's writing about. He doesn't seem to care much if he offends his audience, does he? When he calls the trend of using surnames "frankly ridiculous," he no doubt will offend some readers who have followed this trend. The attitude that comes across in statements like this one helps create the negative tone found in Professor Frop's essay.

This essay serves as a model of how NOT to win over your readers to your opinion. If your tone offends, why should your readers listen to your opinion? In fact, they may not finish reading your essay at all if your tone is rude and **abrasive**.

In this essay there are three main ways the professor offends:

1.   His superior attitude. He reveals this attitude when he says, "When I was naming my children (with a little help from my wife, of course), I chose good, solid names that would be an asset to my children."
2.   His lack of attention to possible legitimate audience arguments to the contrary. For instance, some people choose surnames not to be trendy but to honor family members. He does not acknowledge this—or any other positive arguments for freedom of choice in naming children.
3.   His word choice and name-calling (calls name choices "ridiculous" and "absurd").

Being able to recognize bad tone and separate it from the writer's claims is essential to effectively responding to his or her opinion. If you take the bait and respond with name-calling and an angry attitude in response, you can't have a real discussion.

As Christians, we have an even more important reason for choosing our words carefully. The Bible repeatedly warns believers to use words cautiously. We're not to speak deceitfully. We're to speak gently (Proverbs 15:1-2). We're to speak wisely, weighing our answers before we speak (Proverbs 15:28). Whether written or spoken, our words matter. They can hurt others, or they can edify (I Thessalonians 5:11). So choose your tone carefully. As believers, we're representatives of Christ and his kingdom—something we need to remember each time we speak and write.

CWJ

IN YOUR JOURNAL ▶

Today, we want you to go back through and underline all the words and sentences in red where the professor's tone is offensive. Look particularly for points where the professor's superior attitude and poor word choice affect his tone.

Choose three examples and copy them into your CWJ.

CAPSULE 3

READING TO QUESTION

You've read this essay twice already—once to understand and summarize, and once to try to help you separate the writer's tone from what he's saying. Today we want you to read it again—this time to ask questions.

It seems like a lot to read one essay three times. We know that. However, in order to understand and engage with another writer, you must really know what he's saying and understand where his argument is weak and strong. This often takes multiple readings.

We've said it before. Good writing requires that you be an excellent reader. And the best way to become a better reader is practice. Don't just let your eyes run over the page. Reading closely is a little like dissecting a frog in biology. When you get deep inside you see and understand its structure—you see things that aren't apparent on the surface.

The claim and reasons are the structure, or "bones" of the essay. If these aren't well-formed and strong, that's a big flaw. Being able to "dissect" and find these parts of an essay is essential to responding to it. If you miss a writer's main points because you're distracted by surface features like tone and style, you can't really respond to the essay's message.

CWJ

◀ IN YOUR JOURNAL

In Lessons 2.1 and 2.2, we learned reading to question. Today, we'll combine some of the things we did in capsules 2.1.4 , 2.2.2, 2.2.3, and 2.2.4.

1.   First, read through the essay. As you read, highlight the writer's main claim and the reasons supporting his claim. In your CWJ, write down any questions you think of as you read. Next, think about what you've read. List one or two things you can determine about the writer's worldview from this essay in your CWJ.
2.   Are there any definitions? If so, write them down in your CWJ.
3.   Look at the claim and reasons you highlighted. Does the writer provide any evidence for the claim and the reasons? If so, list the evidence here.
4.   Is the evidence strong or weak? (Hint: can you think of other reasons that are just as convincing for the opposite side?) If so, list your opposing reasons here.

CAPSULE 4

2.3.4

FINDING SHARED ASSUMPTIONS

Even if you don't agree with most of what a writer says, there's almost always something you agree on. For instance, you may disagree with a writer who is in favor of gun control. He may argue in his essay that there should be strict laws on gun ownership. But you both probably agree on a few things:

1.   Guns can be dangerous.
2.   Gun safety is important.
3.   There should be limits on who should be able to own a gun (for example, people with certain types of criminal records or people with certain mental illnesses, etc.).

If you can find these shared assumptions—common ground—you will be better able to have a conversation in your writing.

In some instances, you may have absolutely no common ground or shared assumptions with a writer. But you might be surprised. In most instances, you will share some beliefs with a writer you oppose.

IN YOUR JOURNAL ▶

CWJ

Today, let's take a break from Professor Frop's essay. Instead, look at the two controversial topics below. For each, list two things that the writer and a reader with an opposite opinion can probably agree on, regardless of which side they take on the issue.

1. You should/should not punish children by spanking them.
2. The government should/should not impose stricter laws on junk food to help create healthier Americans.

CAPSULE 5   2.3.5

RESPONDING TO OPINIONS

We hope you're beginning to recognize opinions when you hear or read them. When those opinions come in the forms of claims and reasons in an argument, we hope you're learning to examine the worldview, logic, and evidence that support them.

In the next lesson, we'll tackle writing a response to an opinion. Someday, if your writing gets published, you may occasionally get angry responses to what you say. Not everyone has learned to take apart an argument and examine it. Even grown-ups sometimes respond emotionally rather than logically.

Here are two things to remember that can help diffuse conflict and get the conversation back on track:
1.   As a reader, if you disagree with a writer and would like to express your opinion, respond logically to the argument itself, not with a rude tone full of emotion.
2.   As a writer, respond in a godly manner even when another writer doesn't offer you that same respect.

We'll conclude this lesson with a World Wisdom that will help you think about responses to opinion and how we can gracefully maintain our Christian witness when our writing is attacked.

WORLD WISDOM

WORLD Magazine *writer and editor Marvin Olasky has seen all sorts of letters in his day. Here, he discusses how* WORLD *handles angry responses to writers' opinions:*

A generation ago, one popular commercial showed a man receiving a slap on the face (or slapping himself) and saying, "Thanks, I needed that."

In the Bible, when King David has to flee from Jerusalem because his son has rebelled, a man named Shemei yells insults at David. One of the king's helpers wants to kill Shemei, but David says, "Leave him alone, and let him curse, for the Lord has told him to."

That's why WORLD *has a gentle-answer policy in regard to nasty letters. In part, our reasoning is from Proverbs 15:1, which tells us that "A soft answer turns away wrath…" Many times gentle answers to angry letter-writers have led to gentle responses. But even when that doesn't happen, we sometimes need slaps, and our response almost always is to think that God has us reading the letter for a reason, and to write, "thank you."*

Sometimes we politely challenge readers who make general critiques of a story to tell us how they would have written it. But, tempting though it is, we try not to respond as famous journalist Edward R. Murrow did upon receipt of a particularly foolish letter: "Dear sir, An insane person has stolen your stationery. I thought you'd like to know."

CWJ

Today, look back at the three examples of bad tone you chose from Professor Frop's essay in your CWJ for 2.3.2. How could you change the wording to make the tone inoffensive? Choose two of the sentences and rewrite them in a way that makes them more appealing to the reader and less offensive.

◀ IN YOUR JOURNAL

STYLE TIME

In this unit, we're looking at words people use improperly. Today, we'll look at prepositions that people commonly misuse. Keep track of these wrong preposition errors and others like them in your writing. Log your usage mistakes under the "wrong word" tab in your CWJ. Checking your writing against this list before turning in an assignment will help you to eliminate wrong word errors.

Of for *Have*

This one seems confusing at first: Why would anyone substitute *of* for *have*? If you don't read a lot, you rely on what you hear. People tend to run words together when speaking: *I could have* bought it becomes, "I *could've* bought it." If you are only hearing *could've*—not reading it—it sounds exactly like *could of*.

Some others to watch out for are:

Would have

Should have

Must have

Center *on*, not Center *around*

Think about this one: center *around* isn't logical. You must center *on* it. It's likely that people are getting two expressions mixed up here. You can think the world *revolves* (turns) around you, but it can't center *around* you. The center of something is a fixed place. It doesn't move.

Build *on*, not Build *off of*

This is similar to the previous one: you can build *on* something. How logically would you build *off of* it?

By accident, not *on* accident

We're not sure why people get this one mixed up. Maybe it's because you can do things *on* purpose? However, you do things *by* accident.

Bored *with*, not *of*

This is another one of those usages that you can only learn by hearing and seeing it used properly. Lots of people say they're bored *of* things, but actually, they're bored *with* them.

There are many other common misusages like this one. If you find that you are guilty of any of them, add them to the wrong word section of your CWJ.

Almost everyone has a few, even if you read a lot and have an English teacher for a parent. Both Ron and Jenny grew up with English teacher moms, and yet they heard some things wrong or picked up bad habits from friends. Ron sometimes says something is lying "in the floor" instead of "on the floor." And sometimes Jenny says "would of" instead of "would have." Old habits die hard. Keeping track of your errors will help make you aware of them.

THE RIGHT WORD

 Below are the five vocabulary words in context for this week. You should already have defined them in your journal as you found them in the reading.

1. If you're not careful, how you respond—your tone—can completely **obscure** your message.
2. & 3. Gender-specific names would also eliminate another problem I find particularly **nettling**: the **appropriation** of male names for female use.
4. We designed the professor to be a bit **sanctimonious** and condescending.
5. In fact, they may not finish reading your essay at all if your tone is rude and **abrasive**.

Using your thesaurus, try to find the BEST word to replace the bold word in the sentence. If you aren't familiar with the meanings of all the synonyms for each word in the thesaurus, you may need to use your dictionary to look them up. That way you can choose the word that best fits the sentence.

Write with WORLD

WHAT WRITERS WILL NEED FOR THIS LESSON:

▶ Your writer's journal
▶ Dictionary
▶ Thesaurus
▶ Paper
▶ Highlighter
▶ Colored pen or pencil

CAPSULE 1

2.4.1

FORMING AN OPINION

In the big scheme of things, certain types of opinions don't matter. Some people have opinions on everything—from the time they wake up in the morning till they go to bed at night. The first thing out of this type of person's mouth in the morning might be: "Yellow is too bright for a tablecloth at breakfast time. We need something darker!" Then they'll probably have an opinion about whether Cheerios or Lucky Charms taste better, and so on. You may be this type of person or have someone like this in your family.

When it comes to matters of taste, like what breakfast cereal is more pleasing to the palate or what color best appeals to your eyes at 7 a.m., one opinion isn't superior to another. However, as we begin this lesson, we must remember that when it comes to moral issues, opinions are more than likes and dislikes. Some opinions are right, and some are wrong

WORLD WISDOM

In everything we do—even offering opinions on moral issues—we want to glorify God. So, as *God's World News* editor and writer Rebecca Cochrane reminds us, we need to test our opinions against God's word:

In 1 Thessalonians 5, Paul encourages believers to evaluate everything they hear. Today, information comes at us from all directions. Consciously or unconsciously, we inevitably form opinions. It is important to take an active approach to making those opinions—an approach that allows us to test everything and hold on to what is good.

God alone is the standard for all truth. We who, as Paul also says, "have the mind of Christ" should be careful and diligent to seek to form opinions that are consistent with God's own truth.

So how do we do that?

Obviously, a good knowledge of Scripture is the firmest foundation with which to begin. Next, we should be confident, not in our own thoughts, but in the truth of that Scripture. That gives us the freedom to consider opposing viewpoints—to test them and hold on to what is good.

God is not threatened by other opinions. He is and always will be true. It may be hard for me, though, to hear a criticism about my own thoughts.

Therefore, a humble attitude is important when forming an opinion. It is better for me to learn what is right than it is for me to be right all the time. How much do I really know? Where is my knowledge or experience lacking? Do my thoughts hold up against God's truth? Does an opposing opinion have some merit I should consider?

If my confidence is in God's unchanging truth, then I can evaluate my own opinions as well as those of others who may challenge my position. That challenge should result in greater strength for my own thoughts, if I honestly seek to shape those thoughts according to truth. And thoughts that are taken captive to the obedience of Christ demolish false arguments (2 Corinthians 10:5). So we won't be "tossed back and forth" by the opinions of others (Ephesians 4:14).

The more you read and memorize the Bible, the more steeped in a Christian worldview you will become. In Psalm 1, the Bible tells us we will be blessed if "our delight is in the law of the Lord," which is revealed in Scripture, and if we "meditate on it day and night." Another clear message of the Bible is that knowing God's word brings wisdom.

But even pastors and other Christians who know the Bible well benefit from tools. Books called concordances list all relevant verses under topics like "the heart," "money," "love," and so on. (You might have a short concordance in the back of your Bible that lists a few verses on popular topics.)

The Internet also offers a wealth of tools: biblegateway.com allows you to search several different versions of the Bible. You can find all verses with the word you're looking for in it. You can also find several different Bible concordances online.

As a Christian, your first question when forming an opinion should be, "What does the Bible say about it?" Using tools like these can help you to test your opinions against Scripture.

CWJ

IN YOUR JOURNAL ▶

Today, look back over the three essays we've read in this unit (found in capsules 2.1.3, 2.2.1, and 2.3.1). Which one of these most inspires you to argue with the author? Write a few sentences explaining why.

When you finish, use one of these resources (a concordance or on-line resource) to see what the Bible has to say about the topic of names or heroes. Write down anything interesting that you discover. We'll come back to this later.

CAPSULE 2 2.4.2

WHERE DO YOU AGREE?

Have you ever written a letter to a magazine to share your opinion? What are some reasons you might want to do that? Perhaps the topic of the essay is something you feel strongly about. You feel like the author has missed a key point. Especially if it's an important topic, you want to add to the conversation. Often magazines print a few of these opinions. Your letter helps to continue the conversation and might help readers consider another viewpoint on the issue.

Good conversation—whether in print or the spoken word—helps us to get closer to the truth. If you have something relevant to add to the conversation on a topic, consider expressing it in a short letter to the editor. In this lesson, we'll show you how.

Magazines get lots of letters from "cranks" and hot-headed people who don't really care about learning the truth. In fact, such letter-writers often miss the central idea of the essay or story and focus in on a single statement or phrase that they do not like. These generally do not get printed, since they don't add to the conversation—they're a distraction and a hindrance to seeking truth.

So the first thing you need to remember when writing a letter to the editor is not to get distracted by unimportant details. A good place to start is figuring out where you agree with the writer.

As we discovered in 2.3.4, even if we disagree with an essay as a whole, there are probably some points we agree on. In fact, we might even think the author makes a good point or two. Often our disagreement is not a clear-cut "I'm right and you're wrong." Someone can have a valid claim and reasons, but we might reach different conclusions. Take the idea of a hero, for instance. You might find Mrs. Cheaney's claim and reasons for her definition of a hero to be logical. However, perhaps you've had a personal experience with someone you consider to be a hero. Based on your experience, you might disagree with her definition.

Or perhaps there's very little you agree with. In Professor Frop's essay, for instance, you may find it hard to identify shared assumptions.

Regardless of whether you mostly agree or mostly disagree, beginning with a positive comment is a good way to open your letter.

CWJ

Today, look at yesterday's CWJ. Is this the essay you would most like to write a letter to the magazine about?

If not, decide which one is. When you've made that decision, look through the essay again to see what points you agree with and list them in your journal. Then list anything else that you like about the essay.

CAPSULE 3   2.4.3

WHERE—AND WHY—DO YOU DISAGREE?

In 2.1.2 , we discussed the importance of not being a blank slate. On the opposite end of the spectrum, you don't want to be the type of person who instinctively disagrees and is highly opinionated with no reasons to back your opinions.

It's okay if you don't immediately know why you disagree. A gut feeling is a good place to begin. But remember, it's just a feeling. It's good to begin with an opinion. If it doesn't hold up, it's okay. We're trying to find the truth, not back up our opinion at all costs.

Today, we want you to spend some time in your CWJ. If you're writing about one of the "names" essays, look back at your "doubting" questions (see 2.1.4, and 2.3.3). After you've done this, move on to today's assignment in your CWJ.

CWJ

Skim back over the essay you're writing about in your letter. Do the following:
1.   List the points where you disagree.
2.   For each point where you disagree, ask yourself, "Is there a good reason that supports my opinion?"
Use these questions to evaluate each point of disagreement:
   ▶   Have you had a personal experience that runs counter to what the author says?
   ▶   If you haven't done so already, test your reasons against Scripture. Does the Bible have anything specific to say on the topic that goes against what the author says?
   ▶   Is the author's argument illogical in any way?
3.   Write down your counterarguments.

That's it for today!

WRITING A LETTER TO THE EDITOR

Have you ever seen a section in a newspaper or magazine where readers' letters are published? Usually, these letters either praise or criticize a story or editorial published in an earlier edition. Letter writers may argue with an earlier published opinion from another reader. Letter writers also correct the publication when they've printed an incorrect fact.

Publications like to get letters. It lets newspapers and magazines know that people are reading them. It helps publishers figure out what topics their readers are interested in. It might even make a writer reconsider an opinion and tackle a topic again.

Sometimes, a reader might write a letter to the editor simply to thank them for addressing an interesting topic. That's a worthwhile letter to write; it's always good to say thank you for something you appreciate. Today, though, we want you to write a letter to the editor discussing an article you disagree with. We've been working toward developing a thoughtful opposing opinion and expressing it in writing in this unit. A letter to the editor is a perfect opportunity.

We hope learning this skill will inspire you to begin writing such letters to real publications. If you read as a believer and a skeptic as we've learned in this unit, you will find yourself more interested in conversing with the writers. Letters to the editor are a great way to do so. And who knows, you may even get published!

That's what happened to Joanna Saufley when she read a story in *Trak* magazine. She read an article called "iDolatry," in which writer Daniel Devine interviews pastor and blogger Tim Challies. In the article, Challies discusses his new book, *The Next Story: Life and Faith After the Digital Explosion*. In it, he cautions Christians that technologies such as Facebook can result in people having less face-to-face communication and shallow relationships. Based on her own experience, Joanna disagreed. Here is the letter to the editor she wrote to *Trak*:

Dear Editor,

I enjoy *TRAK* magazine. However, the recent iDolatry article (p.12) from the October issue left me unconvinced. A few things in the article can be easily contradicted.

Immediately in the first paragraph, Challies reports, "the latest technology may represent misplaced affections—and can result in shallow relationships." Personally, a lot of my relationships have grown over communication through Facebook. Former acquaintances are now good friends.

Conversation on Facebook has no awkward "what should I say next" pauses, making it easier to chat with newly met individuals. Communication through Facebook has allowed me to strengthen relationships that otherwise would never have reached such depths. Sometimes, an insignificant topic on Facebook can turn into a deep heartfelt discussion that would not have been kindled without the start of the topic. For example, I am a homeschooler playing on my local school's basketball team. Facebook has sparked a fairly deep conversation between a teammate and me; on the court and sidelines I would not be able to speak with this teammate on the matter.

Another statement I can easily argue is in the second paragraph, "For young people it's more and more natural to have very little face-to-face contact." Although this is the nature of today's lifestyle, Facebook does not cause this. I have been a Facebook user for the past year. Not only do I still prefer face-to-face contact, but communication on Facebook makes me desire to visit friends more often. I would never turn down the opportunity to see someone over having an airwaves chat. Technology provides an easier way to schedule gatherings, which all of my friends greatly anticipate. Since I am homeschooled and live out in the country, I do not have the privilege of seeing my friends every day. Besides, my friends and I are always busy with sports, studies, and other activities, making it hard for us to have face-to-face or phone time. The limited amount of time teenagers have in a day causes them to resort to technology for the quickest way of communication.

A third point that Challies makes is that technology communicators grow content with quick news for entertainment rather than wanting to "ponder" what they read from others and "put it through a Biblical lens." Personally, seeing news on the screen rather than hearing it face to face provides time for me to think before I "speak" instead of feeling compelled to respond on the spot.

In conclusion, technology has enhanced the quantity and quality of my relationships thereby providing a greater opportunity to minister to others at home and abroad. Although I still prefer and seek face-to-face contact, the lack of time has made me content with discussions via Facebook. When I do gather with a friend or two or have the time to write a letter, it is easy to breeze past insignificant topics and dive into the intimate matters of our lives. Thanks, Mr. Challies, for a chance to consider how grateful I am for my Facebook.

Sincerely,
Joanna Saufley

As you dive into writing your own letter today in your CWJ, you can use this letter as a model. You don't necessarily have to have three points, nor does it have to be quite as long. However, I want you to notice three things Joanna does particularly well:

1. Her letter is polite. At the beginning, she tells the editor that she likes *Trak* Magazine. In no place does she seem angry nor does she attack the author. At the end, she thanks him for his work, since it has made her consider how grateful she is for Facebook.

2.   Her letter is organized. She quotes what the author says that she disagrees with. Then she explains why.

3.   Her letter is well-supported. She gives strong personal examples for each of her points, explaining how Facebook has given her deeper, stronger relationships and helped enable spending face-to-face time rather than diminishing it.

This letter isn't perfect. Joanna could, at times, make slightly different word choices to soften her tone. For instance, rather than saying a few of Mr. Challies' points "can be easily contradicted," she might say that "his points may be true for some teens; however, in my personal experience, Facebook has had the exact opposite effect." Overall, though, this is a well-thought-out letter that shows that good readers of any age can become a part of the conversation.

CWJ

Today, you will write your letter to the editor. One great thing about opposing someone else's opinion is that much of the work has already been done for you. Because you have something you are arguing *against*, you don't have to do much work in "thinking up" an argument or planning your organization. He has already structured your argument for you. You simply address the points you disagree with, in the order the writer presented them.

Use your list from the last CWJ (2.4.3). This list should contain most of the material you need. Just make sure that it follows the order of the original article, and you're ready to get started! Here's how:

1.   Begin with a salutation: Dear Editor,

2.   Say something nice about the magazine or share something in the essay that you thought was a good point or agreed with.

3.   Start each paragraph by quoting what the writer said, then explaining why you disagree. Then provide your evidence. This might be a personal example, a scriptural reason for disagreeing, or a reason the argument doesn't make sense to you (is illogical, etc.)

4.   Use strong transitions to get from one idea to the next.

5.   Be mindful of your tone; be as positive as you can about the writing. Never attack the writer or belittle the work she has done. Treat the writer with respect.

6.   Close with another positive statement about the publication or what you gained from reading the essay.

7.   Finish with Sincerely, _____ (your name)

◄ IN YOUR JOURNAL

BEFORE YOU HIT THE SEND KEY . . . .

Just a few years ago, most of the letters we received at *God's World News* came in the regular (snail) mail. Today, we rarely get any comments that arrive in an envelope. Most arrive via e-mail. That's a perfectly acceptable way to send your opinions. However, it makes it easier to dash off a quick letter without putting enough thought into it.

Our advice is to always write it as a document and then cut and paste it into email after you've checked (and rechecked!) it for typographical errors, wrong words, and careful tone. If you're working on a word processor, it will often note spelling errors for you. Most even warn you with some sort of colored underlining if you have a major sentence error such as a problem with subject/verb agreement. Drafting using word processing software can help you catch your mistakes.

It won't catch problems with tone, though. We suggest you set it aside for a while after you've finished. Then come back and read it aloud. You're more likely to "hear" your tone problems after taking a break.

When you believe your letter is in pretty good shape, move on to today's CWJ.

IN YOUR JOURNAL ▶

CWJ

You'll need a hard copy of your letter to work with, so if you've written it on a word processor, print a copy.

Begin by highlighting everything positive you've said about the magazine, the writer, or the essay. Do you have at least a sentence or two at the beginning and end that are positive and show appreciation and respect? If not, find something else nice to say and add it in.

Now read the essay backwards, word by word, starting from the last word. It shouldn't make any sense this way. That's good. We want you to examine each word individually, and having it not make sense helps. If you find any words that sound harsh or belittling, circle them.

Reread the letter, looking especially at the words you circled. Do they seem at all unkind, rude, or belittling when in context? If so, change the word or sentence to make it kinder. Remember what the Bible says: "Let your speech always be gracious, seasoned with salt, so that you may know how you ought to answer each person" (Colossians 4:6).

When you've done all these things, move on to Style Time.

STYLE TIME

In Unit 2, you've begun keeping a "wrong word" section in your CWJ. Today, we want you to compare your letter against this section of your journal.
As a quick review, we worked on wrong word errors that stem from:

▶ Similar spelling and pronunciation, such as than/then and lose/loose
▶ Improper usage, such as lie/lay and farther/further
▶ Confused prepositions, such as bored of (incorrect) instead of bored with (correct)

After your teacher checks your letter, if she finds any wrong word errors, add them to the wrong word section of your CWJ.

THE RIGHT WORD

Read the following sentences and fill in the blank with the best answer.

1. Your on-paper _____ may be different than your in-person one.
    a. persona   b. family   c. friend

2. A person with few opinions might find it difficult to make a _____statement.
    a. neutral   b. decisive   c. calm

3. An obnoxious tone can completely _____your message.
    a. send   b. obscure   c. justify

4. How to handle poorly-behaved children in Sunday School is a particularly _____problem.
    a. nettling   b. easy   c. humorous

5. Professor Ross E. Frop is _____ and smug.
    a. intelligent   b. kind   c. sanctimonious

6. A tone that is rude and _____ often offends readers.
    a. engaging   b. abrasive   c. humorous

7. Often we find the chores we do day after day to be _____.
    a. appetizing   b. mundane   c. fascinating

8. The American flag is a well-known _____ of our country.
    a. emblem   b. mascot   c. pictogram

9.   Long ago, if a child were born on a saint's birthday, the child was given the saint's name and the saint became the child's _____ saint.

    a. favorite   b. despised   c. patron

10. In order to have a discussion with someone on an issue, you must be able to _____ your opinion.

    a. articulate   b. circumlocute   c. impress

11. If something is irritating, gets on your nerves, or gnaws at you, you might say it _____ you.

    a. rankles   b. amazes   c. saddens

12. _____ is a form of obvious, intentional exaggeration.

    a. Lying   b. Metaphor   c. Hyperbole

13. Two half-truths do not _____ the whole truth.

    a. engender   b. constitute   c. dissolve

14. _____ are misleading or unsound arguments.

    a. Delusions   b. Myths   c. Fallacies

15. The _____ of male names for female use makes naming boys difficult.

    a. appropriation   b. failure   c. stockpiling

UNIT 3 / LESSON 1

REVIEWING TEXTS

GOOD OR BAD, LIKE OR DISLIKE: WORKING WITH CRITERIA

CAPSULE 1

3.1.1

LIKE IT OR NOT: YOU HAVE AN OPINION

I really dislike yogurt. That's not to say I haven't tried to like it. I have sampled every different brand and flavor. I've tried it whipped, extra creamy, low-fat, full-fat, with granola, with berries, and even frozen. Every time I attempt to conquer my distaste for this healthy snack, I end up tossing a half-eaten container into the trash. I simply don't think yogurt is very good.

Most people have strong opinions about what kinds of food they do and do not enjoy. The forty-first president of the United States, George H. W. Bush, disliked broccoli so much he banned it from being served on Air Force One! During the Vietnam War, my father became so accustomed to eating old army rations that he learned never to complain about a meal. Even though he is the least picky eater I know, there are two foods he will not eat: tuna fish and stewed tomatoes.

What about you? Is there a food you can't bear to eat?

When I say that I dislike yogurt, I am offering an evaluation of this food. To evaluate something is to judge it. When you express an opinion about anything – a person, an activity, an idea – you are evaluating it. Here are some examples:

▶ Watching golf is boring.
▶ Science is the most interesting school subject.
▶ Eating out is better than eating at home.
▶ Rainy days are depressing.
▶ Making your bed is a waste of time.
▶ Autumn is the best time of year.

Evaluative statements offer a judgment about something's value. As you read the statements above, did you disagree with any of them? I feel contented and relaxed on rainy days – especially if I am cuddled up with a favorite book – so I definitely disagree with the idea that they are depressing. In fact, I would probably initiate a friendly argument if I heard someone say that rainy days are depressing.

Read the statements again. Could you make an argument for or against each of the statements? Definitely. That's because evaluative statements assert a claim that can be argued. To illustrate this point, take a look at some statements that are not evaluations.

▶ Blue is a primary color.
▶ Christmas is on December 25th.
▶ The last meal of the day is dinner.
▶ People do not have wings.
▶ The sun rises in the east.
▶ Coffee contains caffeine.

How is this set of statements different from the previous set? That's right. These statements are facts, not opinions. More than likely, no one will argue that people do have wings or that the sun rises in the east.

In order to be evaluative, statements need to include opinion words. For instance, if you changed the statements to say "Blue is the most beautiful primary color" or "Drinking coffee is pointless unless it is caffeinated," you would be making an evaluation. How could you transform the rest of these facts into evaluative statements?

Evaluations such as this are the driving force behind written arguments. Think about it. You probably don't bother arguing about something unless you have an opinion about whether it is good or bad, helpful or not helpful, worth doing or not worth doing, and so on.

Let's begin this unit by discovering what you are opinionated about.

CWJ

IN YOUR JOURNAL ▶

For the next twenty-four hours, keep your CWJ handy. Each time you make an evaluative statement, or express an opinion out loud or in your mind, record it in your journal. You may want to record statements you hear others make as well, particularly if you strongly agree or disagree with them. (Leave a few lines of space between each statement.)

Look back over what you have recorded.

1.   Determine if the statement is indeed an evaluation by asking yourself if someone might disagree with what you have written down. If so, the statement is an evaluation. If it is NOT a statement someone could argue with you about, cross it out.
2.   Now consider the statements that remain. Take some time to think about *why* you expressed each opinion. Are there specific reasons you like or dislike something? For instance, you may hear a song on the radio and think, "That song is terrible!" But do you dislike the song because it's played on the radio too much, because it sounds just like every other song by that band, or because it gets stuck in your head

and you end up singing it all day? Write down any reasons you can think of that may help explain or clarify your evaluation.

CAPSULE 2

IT'S MORE THAN A FEELING: FORMULATING CRITERIA FOR YOUR OPINIONS

Many opinions are actually gut feelings. Every day we express opinions, or make quick evaluations, without considering the reasons behind those feelings. For instance, like everyone else on the planet, I have a favorite t-shirt. If someone asked me why this t-shirt is my favorite, my response would probably be: "I don't know. I just love it." But if I really thought about it, I could come up with a few reasons why this particular shirt holds a special place in my heart - and my wardrobe.

▶ The material is soft and comfortable.
▶ It fits me perfectly.
▶ I like its basic design and gray and navy blue colors.
▶ I feel happy when I wear it because it reminds me of fun times in college.

My preference for this shirt is connected to a gut feeling I have when I look at it. I like it. But with just a little thought, I can identify at least four logical reasons why I always grab this t-shirt first when it comes out of the laundry.

You see, evaluation often begins with an emotion or feeling. Many times we stop there. But for writers, evaluation involves more than just having an opinion. When we express our opinions in writing, we need to be able to explain those opinions to our audience (1) in order to help them understand why we feel the way we do and (2) perhaps convince them to share our opinion.

To engage in evaluation you need to have three things:

1. An opinion
2. Criteria on which you base your opinion
3. Evidence that supports your opinion

As you saw from your CWJ exercise in 2.1.1, you already have plenty of opinions, so in this lesson we will learn how to establish criteria for your opinions.

First, let's define criteria. Criteria are the standards on which you base your judgment or opinion of something. Confusing? Let's look at an example. Since almost everyone has a favorite t-shirt, it should be easy to come up with some criteria for judging a favorite t-shirt. The reasons I listed for why I love my favorite t-shirt may help us. I have identified one criterion to match each of my reasons.

▶ Is the shirt comfortable?
▶ Does the shirt fit well?
▶ Is the shirt **aesthetically** appealing? (Or does the shirt look good?)
▶ Does the shirt make its wearer feel good?

What other criteria might you add?

The evaluations we make everyday are based on more than just gut feelings. Identifying criteria for our opinions helps us see that we don't simply like or dislike something. We have reasons why we feel that way. And those reasons are based on our beliefs about what makes someone or something good or bad, interesting or boring, attractive or unattractive, and so on.

The culture we live in has many public venues designed for evaluating people and things. Consumer product magazines, most valuable player awards, and television singing competitions all offer rewards for being the "best." The product that best meets the criteria for what makes a good coffee maker will win the magazine's award for this category. The athlete that best meets the criteria for what makes someone valuable to his or her team members will win the most valuable player award. The singer who fails to meet the criteria for what makes someone a "star" will be sent home from the competition. Can you think of any other venues that are used for public evaluation?

Sometimes the criteria for these competitions are unstated, or implicit. For example, the Baseball Writers Association of America, which presents the Most Valuable Player award, does not offer specific criteria for how to judge who is most valuable. Instead, voters get to decide what qualities they think make a player valuable on their own.

Other times the criteria are stated, or explicit. An example of explicit criteria can be found in Titus 1:5-9 where God provides a list of criteria for selecting the elders, or leaders, of the church. A few of the criteria for judging a person's ability to serve as an elder include:

▶ Are his children obedient?
▶ Is he faithful to his wife?
▶ Is he hospitable?
▶ Is he self-controlled?
▶ Does he encourage others with right thinking and **rebuke** those who persist in wrong thinking?

Identifying explicit criteria is a useful activity for writers because (1) it helps us to more fully understand why we hold a certain opinion and (2) gives us the tools we need to explain and defend our opinion to an audience.

WORLD WISDOM

Identifying criteria upfront helps writers narrow the scope of their research and select a topic. Music writer for *WORLD Magazine*, Arsenio Orteza, approaches his professional assignments by first thinking about criteria.

"During the 21 years that I've written about music and musicians in WORLD, the number-one requirement, or criteria, for what I write about is that it be newsworthy. "Newsworthy" can mean "at the top of the bestseller charts" (Lady Gaga, Justin Bieber) or simply being worthy of headlines (Korn's guitarist's becoming a Christian, the Beach Boys' SMiLE finally coming out four decades after it was supposed to). Frankly, as newsworthiness happens on its own, it's the easy part.

Sometimes, though, it doesn't happen at all, at which point I seek out new music that simply teaches me something. That something can be harmony and counterpoint (Bach, Stravinsky), the convergence of Europe and Africa in America (Miles Davis, Wynton Marsalis), or the ironies resulting from being in the world but not of it (too many gifted singer-songwriters to mention—although Bob Dylan, Loudon Wainwright III, and They Might Be Giants rank near the top of that list).

But mostly I try to be pleasantly surprised. So I listen to as much music in as many different genres as possible. I also scour numerous music-related websites on a daily basis, looking for connections between what people are interested in and what I can tolerate listening exclusively to for a few weeks.

Sometimes I even get to meet and interview the people behind the music. Almost all of them are pleasant and grateful to be chatting up their latest project with someone who's knowledgeable about and interested in it. Overall: most cool."

CWJ

Part A

Orteza offers us at least four examples of criteria he uses to help him identify the subject for his next piece.

◀ **IN YOUR JOURNAL**

▶   Is the music/musician newsworthy?
▶   Does the music/musician teach me something?
▶   Are people interested in the music/musician?
▶   Would I enjoy listening to only this music/musician for an extended period of time?

1.   Suppose Orteza enlists your help selecting a subject for his newest article. What criteria might you add to his? In other words, are there any other criteria that could help you determine what artist or type of music would make an interesting topic for a magazine article? Brainstorm at least two additional criteria.
2.   Based on these criteria, (Orteza's and yours), identify a musician or music genre to write about.

Explain how your choice meets the criteria. (Remember, it need not meet all of the criteria, but enough that your audience will be able to understand why you made this choice.)

Part B

Select two items from the following list. Brainstorm a list of three or four criteria someone might use to judge each item. We'll do more with these lists in 3.1.3.

▶ hamburger
▶ tennis shoes
▶ beach
▶ pillow
▶ sports team
▶ lip balm
▶ pet
▶ university
▶ friend

CAPSULE 3

DON'T STOP THERE: REFINING CRITERIA BASED ON REASON AND AUDIENCE

Now that you've had some practice developing criteria on your own, let's move to the next step: refining criteria. Once you come up with criteria, you need to make sure that your criteria will seem reasonable to other people.

Take, for example, our discussion of favorite t-shirts in 3.1.2. Do you think most people would agree that the criteria we came up with are acceptable criteria for judging a t-shirt? Probably so. Most people will judge a shirt based on qualities such as how comfortable it is, how well it fits, how it looks, and how it makes them feel. But what if we included these criteria?

▶ Does it have long sleeves?
▶ Is it a shirt from a rock concert or political rally?
▶ Is it free of holes or other signs of wear?

Why do you think people might object to these criteria? Exactly. They are too specific. I've never gotten a t-shirt from a rock concert or political rally, but I do have a favorite t-shirt. In fact, my favorite t-shirt is short-sleeved and has several small holes in it. (It has been worn a lot, after all.) So if someone argued that a favorite t-shirt had to be long-sleeved, from a rock concert or political rally, and free of signs of wear, I might not find their argument persuasive. These criteria would not be convincing to me.

Since our goal in writing is to explain our ideas to others in a convincing manner, as we develop criteria, we also have to be mindful of the audience we are writing for. Being aware of your audience is an important part of refining your criteria.

For example, imagine you are writing an evaluation of a local water park. What criteria might you come up with if you were writing your review for a group of middle-schoolers who are planning a field trip?

▶ How long is the average wait to go on a ride?
▶ Is there a good mix of water slides, roller coasters, and activity pools?
▶ Are the rides appropriate for teenage guests, or are they too childish?
▶ Were students who have been to the water park before pleased with their experience?

How might your criteria be different if you were writing an evaluation of the same water park for parents who are considering allowing their children to go on the field trip?

▶ Are there an adequate number of well-trained life guards?
▶ Does the park have an acceptable "track record" for safety on rides?
▶ Are the facilities clean and sanitary?
▶ Does the water park have a good reputation among community members?

Of course, some of the criteria might overlap. For instance, middle-schoolers might be interested in having clean bathrooms too, but that would probably be a much more important concern for a parent. Parents might want to know that the water park had age-appropriate activities for their child, but the safety of the rides would likely be higher on their priority list. We can probably agree that all of the criteria we have listed are reasonable, but some will be more convincing to particular audiences.

So, as you refine your criteria, you should ask yourself two questions:
1. Are these criteria reasonable to most people?
2. Which criteria would be most convincing to my specific audience?

THE PROFESSOR'S OFFICE:

Every year universities across the nation receive applications from thousands of would-be students. For some public universities, the number of applications reaches into tens of thousands. How do university officials make decisions about who is admitted to the school and who isn't? Criteria.

Admissions officers use criteria such as grades, standardized test scores, class rank, and the rank of the high school a student attended to determine if that student is a good candidate for their university. These are all forms of quantitative criteria, or criteria that can be measured in some way. Making admission decisions would be quick and easy if universities relied solely on quantitative criteria. The people with the highest scores and rankings would be the first to get a spot.

But universities also employ qualitative criteria to evaluate applicants. Students are asked to offer information about their extracurricular activities, include teacher recommendation letters, and write essays as part of their college applications. Qualitative criteria are harder to judge since they can't be counted or charted on a graph, but they offer another valuable perspective on a student's ability. For example, they can show admissions officers more about a student's passions and interests than a score on a test can.

Both quantitative and qualitative criteria are useful and together they present a fuller picture of the object or person being judged, in this case high school seniors.

Though you probably won't be admitting anyone to college in the near future, you can learn from this university practice. Whenever you evaluate something, try to base your opinion on a mix of quantitative and qualitative criteria. If you are evaluating a band, ask how many records it has sold (quantitative criterion) and also ask about the band's impact on popular culture (qualitative criterion). Since people are swayed by different kinds of evidence, basing your evaluation on both types of criteria will make your argument more convincing to more people.

CWJ

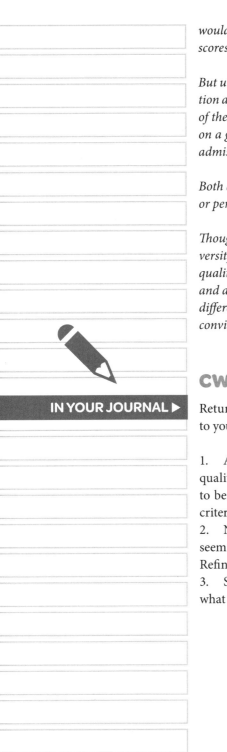

IN YOUR JOURNAL ▶

Return to your CWJ exercise from 3.1.2 for some practice refining criteria to make it more convincing to your audience.

1.   As you read through the criteria you came up with for each item, note whether it is quantitative or qualitative. Remember that quantitative criteria can be measured or counted and qualitative criteria have to be explained with words. Refine your criteria to include a mix of both quantitative and qualitative criteria.

2.   Now share the criteria you have identified with another person. Ask if the criteria you have listed seem reasonable to them. Ask if there are any criteria you didn't mention that they think are important. Refine your criteria based on their input.

3.   Select one specific audience for your evaluation of each item. Refine your criteria again based on what kinds of information you think would be most important to that particular audience.

WORKING BACKWARDS: IDENTIFYING IMPLICIT CRITERIA

By now, we have expressed individual opinions about the food we eat, the clothes we wear, the music we listen to, and the activities we engage in. We have also discussed larger, public forums of evaluation—such as television singing competitions—where the entire nation gets involved in offering a collective opinion.

In this capsule, we are going to focus on evaluations that take place at the local level—in your hometown. Think about it for a moment. Do you have strong opinions when it comes to your hometown?

I know I do. Recently, I visited some friends in their hometown. They gleefully took me out to the "best" Mexican food restaurant in town. They proudly bragged that this cuisine was much more authentic than the food one finds in other parts of the state. It was good, but in my opinion it didn't hold a candle to a certain Mexican food restaurant where I live. When I compared the two establishments, I determined that at "my" restaurant the salsa and chips were tastier, the meat was of better quality, the atmosphere was more inviting, and the wait for a table wasn't nearly as long. I concluded that the restaurant in my hometown was definitely preferable to this one. (I bet you can easily identify the criteria I used to form my opinion here!)

The truth is we all have opinions about what's "best" about our own hometowns. Think back to a time when you had out-of-town guests. Where did you take them to eat? Where did you go for entertainment or sight-seeing? What did you tell them they had to experience before they returned home? Answering these questions should help you identify some of the things that you consider special about your hometown.

But what about people who visit your city without a personal tour guide such as yourself? Most cities publish a document called a visitor's guide. These guides are divided into categories such as "eating out," "nightlife," "historical attractions," and "family fun" that list what the city has to offer its visitors. While visitor's guides provide information about what there is to do or see in a city, they don't usually spend much time evaluating which offerings are better than others. They are meant to be informative rather than evaluative.

Periodically, local magazines will publish "best of" issues that judge which establishments really are the "best" in their particular category. The announcement of each winner is followed by a blurb explaining what qualities make it the clear choice. Though the criteria are often unstated, they can usually be in-ferred from the winner's write-up. Consider this description of the "best public library":

The Southeast Public Library has earned the title "best public library." Located squarely in downtown, the library can be accessed easily by public and private modes of transportation. This beautiful historic building houses an interior that is anything but **antiquated***. Patrons enjoy all the modern amenities necessary for a comfortable reading and researching experience, including plush couches, polished wooden tables, and soft lighting. Let's not forget the lavish coffee bar, stocked with delicious pastries and gourmet sandwiches, where book lovers can find something sweet or savory to sink their teeth into. But what is a library really about? The books. This public library contains an impressive collection of popular contemporary and rare-book offerings with an even more remarkable digital collection. A state-of-the-art theater showing documentaries on the hour and a whimsical children's section, complete with a Mother Goose-costumed librarian, confirm this library is a place for the whole family to enjoy.*

After reading the blurb, what criteria do you think the judges based their decision on? Here are a few possibilities:

▶ Is the library easily accessible to all patrons?
▶ Is it a comfortable place to read and research?
▶ Does it have an extensive book collection?
▶ Is it appealing to children and families?
▶ Are there additional amenities (other than books) that make the library an enjoyable destination?

These are just a few of the criteria we could have identified based on the write-up, but you get the idea. **Savvy** readers can work backward from a written evaluation to identify what criteria the writer used to make his or her judgment.

CWJ

Hopefully by now you are inspired to think about what is the "best" in your hometown.

Pretend you are the writer for a local magazine that is publishing a "best of" issue. Identify five categories you want to evaluate. For each category, list four or five criteria that could help you make your judgment and select a winner. When you are finished, you should have five different lists of criteria.

STYLE TIME

 Descriptive phrases called modifiers add interest and specificity to your writing. But when they are incorrectly placed, these phrases may **confound** your readers rather than impress them. Simply make sure these phrases are situated next to the part of the sentence they describe and your readers will thank you.

Misplaced:

While window shopping, a dozen hot dogs flew past my head.

Problem:

Are the hot dogs window shopping?

Correct:

While window shopping, I noticed a dozen hot dogs fly past my head.

Misplaced:

Penelope startled her mother wearing a banana suit and singing at the top of her lungs.

Problem:

Is Penelope's mother wearing a banana suit and singing?

Correct:

Wearing a banana suit and singing at the top of her lungs, Penelope startled her mother.

Penelope, wearing a banana suit and singing at the top of her lungs, startled her mother.

Misplaced:

Rotund and sluggish in appearance, children mistakenly believe the hippopotamus is friendly rather than ferocious.

Problem:

Are the children rotund and sluggish?

Correct:

Children mistakenly believe the hippopotamus, rotund and sluggish in appearance, is friendly rather than ferocious.

REVISE

Each of the sentences below contains a misplaced modifier. Read each sentence, identify the problem, and correct it.

▶ Located squarely in downtown, public and private modes of transportation have easy access to the library.

► With plush couches, polished wooden tables, and soft lighting, patrons enjoy all the modern amenities necessary for a comfortable reading and researching experience.

► Let's not forget the lavish coffee bar where book lovers stocked with delicious pastries and gourmet sandwiches can find something sweet or savory to sink their teeth into.

Now, refer back to the "best public library" paragraph in this capsule to see correct versions of these sentences. How were the sentences you wrote similar to or different from the writer's? (Remember, there is more than one way to correct each of the sentences. And no peeking until after you write your sentences!)

CAPSULE 5 3.1.5

WHY IT'S THE BEST: FINDING EVIDENCE TO SUPPORT YOUR OPINION

By the time you finish with today's capsule, you will have written your own evaluative piece! Let's get started.

First, refer back to the five categories you identified in your CWJ. You are going to pick one of these categories for your "best of" article. But how do you choose? As you begin any piece of writing, there are a few questions you can ask yourself to help you select a topic:

1. Which topic am I most knowledgeable or passionate about?
2. Which topic would I like to learn more about?
3. Which topic would be most interesting to an audience?

Whichever category stood out to you as you asked yourself these questions is probably a good choice. Start with that one and if you need to switch categories later, that's okay.

Now that you have selected the category you want to work with, rewrite the criteria you came up with for that category in your CWJ. You only identified a few criteria in 3.1.4, but since you have narrowed your topic, you'll need a few more criteria to work with. See if you can double what you have and identify ten criteria for your category. As you are thinking of criteria, it may be helpful to ask yourself:

What makes a good _____ (playground, bus stop, barber, slice of pizza)?

Now you can guess the next step, can't you? Refine your criteria. Do you remember the two questions we asked to help us refine our criteria in 3.1.3?

1. Are these criteria reasonable to most people?
2. Which criteria would be most convincing to my specific audience?

This step will require you to identify a specific audience for your written piece. Consider who might be most interested in or who might benefit from the information you have to share. For example, teenagers, parents of young children, or people with a sweet tooth might be a better audience for the category "best milkshake" than health-conscious individuals.

My criteria for "best milkshake" addressed to an audience of parents of young children might include:

▶ Does the establishment offer multiple milkshake sizes including a size that is manageable for small hands?
▶ Is the milkshake a good value? Do you get a lot of milkshake for your money?
▶ Are there several varieties of flavors are offered?
▶ Are there any unique milkshakes that are not offered anywhere else?
▶ Is the milkshake made of quality ingredients?
▶ Is the texture of the milkshake thick and creamy?
▶ Is the establishment kid-friendly? (bright décor, family bathrooms, high chairs, etc.)
▶ Are there offerings to entice parents such as gourmet add-ins or "nostalgic" milkshakes from their childhood?
▶ Do kids actually drink the milkshake or does it end up in the trash?
▶ How many milkshakes does the establishment sell each day?

Now that you have a category and criteria decided upon, it's time to conduct your research. You may already have an idea of what you think the "best" in your category is, but in order to be a thorough journalist, you are going to have to do some fieldwork.

As we learned in 3.1.2, there are three elements of an evaluation:

1. An opinion
2. Criteria on which you base your opinion
3. Evidence that supports your opinion

Field research will lead you to the third element you need to engage in a thorough evaluation: evidence.

Identify at least three contenders for your category. For example, if I were researching who made the best milkshake in town, I would come up with a minimum of three places to sample. Make a copy of your criteria questions for each contender, leaving space in between each question for jotting down notes. The answers to these questions will serve as the evidence you use to justify your opinion. Get out in the field and let the fun begin!

IN YOUR JOURNAL ▶

CWJ

You should have three sets of answered criteria at this point. Now you have to make sense of the data you have collected.

1.   Read through each set of answered criteria and make an evaluation. Which contender best fulfilled your criteria? That is your winner.
2.   Write a short blurb for the magazine identifying the winner and telling why this contender won. In other words, what evidence did you find that this is indeed the best _____? There's probably no need to address all of your criteria. Pick a few of the most convincing and focus on those. You may want to model your paragraph (or two) on the public library write-up in 3.1.4.
3.   Revise your piece by hunting for sentences with misplaced modifiers and rewriting them.

THE RIGHT WORD

 You have learned five new vocabulary words in this unit. Grab your thesaurus and figure out the best synonym for each word in bold. You may need to look up the synonyms if you aren't sure of their exact meaning. Here are the words as they appear in context.

1.   Is the shirt **aesthetically** appealing?
2.   Can he encourage others with right thinking and **rebuke** those who persist in wrong thinking?
3.   The beautiful historic building houses an interior that is anything but **antiquated**.
4.   **Savvy** readers can work backward from a written evaluation to identify what criteria the writer used to make his or her judgment.
5.   But when they are incorrectly placed, these phrases may **confound** your readers rather than impress them.

Write with WORLD

REVIEWING TEXTS

EVALUATING A CURRENT EVENT

CAPSULE 1

3.2.1

KEEPING "CURRENT" WITH YOUR OPINIONS

Grab a pen or your computer because we are going to start this capsule with a little directed freewriting. Remember that a freewrite is not the time to worry about spelling, punctuation, wording, or even complete sentences. Your only goal here is to get your thoughts down on paper – or the computer screen – so you have material to work with. Here we go:

▶ When you hear the phrase "current events," what words, ideas, or images come to mind?
▶ How knowledgeable are you about current events? Rate yourself on a scale from one (not knowledgeable at all) to five (extremely knowledgeable). Why did you rate yourself this way?
▶ Write down five headings: (1) family, (2) school/church, (3) local, (4) national, and (5) global. Under each heading, jot down what current events you are aware of at the present moment. In other words, what is happening in your family, your classroom or church community, your city, your nation, and your world right now?

Now look back over what you have written. Which heading did you come up with the most current events for? Which heading gave you the most trouble?

Perhaps you are accustomed to thinking of current events as something happening in a foreign country that you get a glimpse of on the five o'clock news. But really a current event is any event of significance taking place at the present moment. Changing jobs, choosing a pet, and moving to a new house are current events that might happen within a family. Getting a new principal or pastor, removing sodas from the cafeteria vending machines, and sponsoring a "fun run" are current events that might take place at school or church. Political elections, natural disasters, and grass roots protest movements all constitute current events at the local, national, and global levels.

Sometimes current events may seem so distant from your own life – especially if they are taking place half a world away – that you find it difficult to have an opinion about them. But as citizens of God's world, it is important that we pay attention to what He is doing in this world and learn to evaluate current events through a biblical worldview. In this lesson, you will learn how to analyze a current event, formulate an opinion about that event, and express your opinion in writing.

WORLD WISDOM

Take a look at what Joel Belz has to say about how a writer develops and tests his opinions.

It's widely held, in both academic and journalistic circles, that anyone trying to write a piece expressing a personal opinion should start out with no opinion at all. I would suggest that such an approach is so overly sanitized—and even sterile—that it will never do anyone much good.

Instead, I suggest that it's far more useful to get into the habit of starting out with an opinion—even a fairly vigorous opinion—and then proceed by challenging that opinion from just as many perspectives as possible. If it holds up, terrific. If it falls by the wayside, that's OK too, because it's truth that we're after.

*Physical scientists use this approach all the time. They don't just start off with a blank slate. They start instead with something they call a hypothesis. And they train themselves to challenge and test those hypotheses in all sorts of ways. They have to be very careful not to twist or warp the evidence, but to observe it carefully and in a balanced manner. The result might be the **affirmation** of some truth, or might be the denial of some falsehood. Either way, the scientist has helped the discussion.*

Writers need to train themselves to approach the discovery of truth in a similar manner. There's nothing wrong with forming an early opinion or hypothesis—so long as you are genuinely ready to see contrary evidence just as quickly as you note affirming evidence.

It's easy, for example, when you're reporting on a meeting or conference or gathering of people to begin forming mental opinions of the speakers and participants as "good guys" and "bad guys"—the people you think are pushing things in a good direction, and the people you don't think of so positively. There's nothing wrong with forming such opinions so long as then you're very careful to keep challenging your early opinions with continuing evidence on both sides of the question.

Indeed, if you use this approach of forming an early hypothesis and then challenging it—but only rarely changing your opinion—then maybe you need to back off a bit and be even harder on those early opinions. All of us need to change our minds from time to time. If we don't find ourselves doing that, at least now and then, we may be more hard-headed than we thought we were!

CWJ

After reading Mr. Belz's piece, answer the following questions in your CWJ.

1.   In this piece, Mr. Belz suggests that writers should approach their work similarly to physical scientists. What do you think he means by this?
2.   Once you have an opinion on something, do you find it easy or difficult to change that opinion? Explain.
3.   Why do you think it is important to be willing to challenge and even change your opinions?

◀ **IN YOUR JOURNAL**

CAPSULE 2

3.2.2

CHANGE IS GOOD: ALTERING YOUR OPINION BASED ON EVIDENCE

Let's return to the freewrite you did in 3.2.1. As you reread each entry, write "opinion" next to the current events you already have an opinion about and "neutral" next to the events you do not have an opinion about. Did you notice any trends in your labeling?

If you are like most people, you are probably more opinionated about current events that concern you – those you listed under the headings family, school, and church – than those that are less closely connected to your life. But as Mr. Belz reminded us in his piece, even if writers do start out with a strong opinion on an issue, they should be willing to alter their opinions based on evidence.

Take a look at how one writer's opinion about her school's plan to build an academic enrichment garden changed after she spent some time researching and analyzing this current event.

This spring our school hopes to begin construction on the Academic Middle School Learning Garden. If you are like me, you probably read that sentence and asked yourself, "Why?" Aren't gardens places where little old ladies grow petunias or your parents take you to walk around and look at a bunch of boring plants? Why in the world would we need a garden at school? And what is there to learn from a garden anyway?

The official proposal filed with the school board states that this outdoor garden will be cultivated on school grounds "for the purpose of enriching the classroom experience and offering an innovative learning model"; therefore, it will be available to and tended by all teachers and students. The garden will start out small with a modest variety of native plants and easy-to-grow vegetables. The plan is to expand the garden each year, eventually incorporating medicinal plants and a wide variety of produce for students to sample.

Stop here for a moment. Turn to your CWJ and write down your opinion of the idea of creating a school garden. Don't worry if you don't know anything about school gardens. Just write down your gut feeling. Then read on.

To be honest, when I first heard about the plan, I was not a fan of the idea. Personally, I would rather our school invest time and money into something more useful like a gigantic trampoline or indoor ice skating rink. At least students would enjoy those things. And these activities would promote physical activity too, which is something adults seem to think is pretty important. But after speaking with some knowledgeable people and doing a little research into the concept, I must admit that I have gained a different perspective. A school garden may not be my first choice – see my other suggestions above – but it's definitely not a bad one.

*You may be surprised to hear that the idea of a school garden isn't new. In fact, there is a **precedent** for these gardens at other schools in the nation. Just do a quick Internet search with the term "school garden" and you will get nearly two million hits. From Hawaii to Maine and from preschools to high schools, educators are getting interested in building gardens. There are also several organizations dedicated to helping administrators and students implement these programs at their schools by providing information about designing and building the gardens, getting students and parents involved, and maintaining the gardens once they are established. There are even books published on the subject! This isn't just an idea our school came up with. Schools have been growing gardens for awhile–and it seems to be working.*

*Principal Parker, one of the garden's most vocal **proponents**, argues that a school garden will have benefits beyond the classroom. When I spoke with him, he explained that school gardens benefit students by introducing them to new food sources and teaching them about nutrition in a hands-on manner. I have to admit that I never liked tomatoes until I helped my mom grow some in our backyard, and I tasted them fresh from the soil. Now I eat them all the time. It seems that, like me, most students are more willing to try food that they have a hand in growing. Parker explains, "School gardens promote a healthier student body, and everyone can get excited about that!"*

Although the cost for building and maintaining the garden will be substantial, there are ways to minimize costs. This is a significant consideration since many parents may not be thrilled to hear that the school is spending funds on a garden when our classrooms are overcrowded and our books are outdated. The Garden Committee Research Report points out that there are dozens of grants available for schools to receive government and non-profit assistance for their gardens. Other ideas in the report for offsetting costs include "doing fundraising projects to raise money, selling the garden's produce to help pay for new seeds and maintenance, and getting local gardeners to volunteer their time and skills."

A survey conducted by the Student Council found that the student body is divided with 47% of students favoring the plan and 53% questioning its worth. If majority rules, then the school garden project may never get a chance to grow. I'm not entirely convinced that a learning garden is the best place to commit limited school funds, but I do think that students and parents need to consider this option very seriously. Who knows? We all might learn something in the process.

How did this writer's opinion, or evaluation, of the proposed school garden change?

She offers her revised stance in at least two places. In the second paragraph, she writes, *"A school garden may not be my first choice – see my other suggestions above – but it's definitely not a bad one."* In the final paragraph, she also offers an assessment: *"I'm not entirely convinced that a learning garden is the best place to commit limited school funds, but I do think that students and parents need to consider this option very seriously."*

Notice that her evaluation did not change from completely disagreeing to completely agreeing with the idea. An evaluation need not be "for" or "against." And a change in opinion need not be total.

Instead, the writer was initially bored with the idea, but through the process of evaluation she became more interested in the project. At the end of the article, she admits she isn't totally convinced, but she is more willing to consider the idea and acknowledge the potential benefits.

How did she come to this conclusion? She did research. And the research she conducted was based on criteria, or what she wanted to find out about the garden project. Remember that criteria are important because they help you identify what you are looking for. They provide the focus for your research.

What criteria do you think the writer used to focus her research of this current event? In other words, what questions did she ask to get started? Here are a few possible criteria:

▶ What is a school garden?
▶ What will creation of a school garden entail?
▶ What do historical or contemporary examples of school gardens tell us about the project's chances for success?
▶ What are the potential benefits of a school garden? (Or who stands to benefit?)
▶ What are the potential drawbacks of a school garden? (Or who stands to lose?)
▶ What is public opinion of the proposal? (administrators, teachers, parents, students)

These criteria led the writer to sources. The sources led her to evidence. And the evidence led her to a revised opinion.

IN YOUR JOURNAL ▶

CWJ

In this capsule, the writer of the school garden piece offers an evaluation of a current event taking place within her sphere of activity and influence. We have already identified several potential criteria she may have used to focus her research. Now we will look at where the criteria led her and how they influenced her final evaluation.

Grab your CWJ and answer these questions:

1.   What sources did the writer mention in her evaluation? Can you think of any other potential sources that the writer did not include?
2.   What evidence did she include that supported the idea of a school garden?
3.   What evidence did she include that was opposed to the idea?
4.   After reading this piece, what is your opinion of the school garden project? Is it different from the opinion you wrote down before reading the piece?
    a.   If it is different, explain why you changed your opinion. What evidence was the most convincing to you?
    b.   If it is the same – and it is okay if it is the same – explain why your opinion did not change. What kinds of evidence might have been more convincing to you?

CAPSULE 3   3.2.3

SEARCHING AND RESEARCHING: LET YOUR CRITERIA BE YOUR GUIDE

As the student's article about a proposed school garden demonstrates, an intelligent evaluation of a current event doesn't just label it as "good" or "bad." Rather, in order to perform an adequate evaluation, writers need to:

1.   Identify criteria (questions) to guide their research
2.   Find sources that offer a variety of viewpoints about the current event
3.   Formulate an opinion based on the information in their sources
4.   Use source evidence to support that opinion

In the remainder of this lesson, you will complete these four tasks and engage in your own evaluation of a current event.

But before you jump in, you must first choose an event. To make your choice, go back to the freewrite you completed in 3.2.1. Circle the current events you wrote down that most interest you.

If you aren't thrilled with the options you identified, check out *Top Story* magazine, the front page of the morning paper, or the home page of a reputable news website. You may also want to ask your parents what current events they are aware of.

During your search, don't spend a lot of time reading articles. Rather, look for headlines that interest you. You'll have plenty of time to research later, and you don't want to devote time to researching events you aren't going to write about. Instead, read only the first paragraph or two of an article if you need more information to make a decision.

Select TWO events to research further. You may have one that you prefer, but go ahead and pick a second one. Research is an unpredictable task. While you may be interested in an event, once you begin to research, you may find very few sources to help you and need to abandon your first choice. If you have more than one option, you won't have to start over completely.

Time to do some pre-writing. Write down your first current event choice as a heading. Underneath the heading, write:

1. Everything you currently know about the event (without doing research)
2. What questions you have about the event (what you DON'T know)
3. Your opinion of the event

Do this for your second current event as well.

Look back through what you have written for both events and highlight the questions you wrote down. These questions will serve as the initial criteria to provide focus for your research.

CWJ

1. In your CWJ, write down the criteria questions you highlighted, leaving space between them for answers. (If you come up with more questions as you search, be sure and add those as well.)

2. Now that you have criteria to guide your research, it's time to get started. Online sites will probably be a major source of your research. You will need to identify three or four helpful sources for BOTH of your current events. Here are some tips:

▶ Choose specific search terms and vary them if necessary. For instance, I could type "malaria vaccine" into my search engine. This would give me over one million hits. If I specify my search by placing "malaria vaccine Africa" in quotation marks, this brings up only four thousand hits, a much more manageable number.

▶ Look for sources that offer different viewpoints about your event. I could search newspapers and news sites for articles about the malaria vaccine, but I would also want to look for opinions from

◀ IN YOUR JOURNAL

doctors and medical associations, charitable organizations working on malaria prevention, and the World Health Organization.

▶ Pay attention to the sources used by the authors of articles you read. They can lead you to your next source!

3. Print out and quickly skim all of your sources. Now it's time to make a choice. Based on the sources you have found, which event do you want to evaluate? (Set aside the sources you found for the second event in case you hit a snag and need to switch later on.)

4. With your criteria close by, read through the sources related to your chosen event. When you come across information that addresses any of your questions, mark it with a highlighter. Once you have read and highlighted your sources, write down answers to your criteria questions in your CWJ. (Make sure to note which source you got the information from in parentheses. Place words and phrases that are directly from the source in quotation marks so you will remember they aren't your own.)

We'll use these answers to summarize the event and formulate an informed opinion in the next capsule.

STYLE TIME: WRONG VERB FORM

 A common mistake writers make when it comes to verbs is using the wrong verb form. English has many irregular verb forms, so picking the right one can be problematic.

Regular verbs follow this pattern:

Present Tense	Past Tense	Past Participle
climb	climbed	climbed
dance	danced	danced
look	looked	looked
paint	painted	painted

Adding the "ed" ending to a present tense verb is the common way to change a verb's tense.

If you have a younger sibling or have been around a child who is learning to talk, you may have noticed that children add "ed" to almost every verb because they haven't learned the irregular forms yet.

That's why you'll hear your little brother say things like:

Yesterday I swimmed at the pool.
I throwed the ball to my friend.
Daddy taked me to work with him.

We laugh at kids when they make these mistakes, but it's not as cute to say or write the wrong verb form when you get older. It's important to learn the irregular forms so you can avoid making embarrassing mistakes.

Some irregulars follow a predictable pattern:

Present Tense	Past Tense	Past Participle
blow	blew	blown
know	knew	known
grow	grew	grown
throw	threw	thrown
fly	flew	flown

But there are just as many irregulars that don't follow any pattern:

Present Tense	Past Tense	Past Participle
take	took	taken
awake	awoke	awoken
think	thought	thought
swing	swung	swung
bid	bid	bid
eat	ate	eaten

As they hear the language more and more, children eventually stop adding "ed" to all verbs and learn irregulars by ear. But most of us still have a few verbs that continue to give us trouble.

I know "swing" is one of my trouble words, which causes a problem since I spend a lot of time at the park with two little kids!

To help you memorize the irregular verbs that give you a problem, dedicate a page in your CWJ to "Troublemaker Verbs." If you can't remember if it's "bring, brang, brung" or "bring, brought, brought," look up the proper usage in a grammar handbook and write it down. Then you can refer to your list when you need to use one of those pesky troublemakers in your writing.

(And, just so you know, it's "bring, brought, brought.")

IT'S TIME FOR A RECAP: LEADING READERS TO YOUR OPINION

Have you ever started watching a television series in the middle of the season? Without any knowledge of the characters or their situations, you are likely to give up on the show before you make it through one episode. What do television producers do to keep this from happening? They start each show with a short summary of the previous episode. This summary is designed to offer enough information for viewers who have never seen the show to be able to follow along with the current episode.

Now, imagine how lost your readers would be if you launched into your current event evaluation without giving them any background. Like the television viewers, they too might be tempted to give up. How do you prevent this from happening? The summary.

Read through the first two paragraphs of the school garden article in 3.2.2. The writer admits she doesn't know anything about school gardens before she conducts research. Accordingly, she assumes that her readers may not know much either, so she spends time at the beginning of her piece explaining what the learning garden project is about.

Notice how much information she provides in her short summary. In just three sentences, the writer offers us information to explain what a school garden is, what elements it will include, and who will maintain it.

Look at the sources you found, and you will probably find summaries of the basic facts of the event near the beginning of the piece. In journalistic articles, these summaries may be as short as one sentence. Journalists work from the assumption that their audience may have no knowledge of their subject prior to reading. Because they have strict word limits, journalists must quickly provide background material so their readers will have a shared understanding to work from.

For instance, the article "Malaria Vaccine—A Really Big Deal" from *Top Story* magazine begins with this helpful summary of the malaria problem.

> Most mosquito bites usually cause a little itching and discomfort. But in some parts of the world, a mosquito bite can mean death. Malaria is a disease carried by mosquitoes. When an infected mosquito bites, parasites enter the body and attack red blood cells. If it is not treated, malaria quickly becomes life threatening. A million people die from malaria every year, and most of them are children.

Very quickly this author has told us what malaria is and the problem it poses. Now we can begin to understand why a vaccine could be "a really big deal." Once you have established a shared understanding such as this, readers will be primed and ready for your opinion.

Sometimes our opinions can appear pretty black and white. We dislike going to the dentist. We like going to the movies. We believe brushing one's teeth is a good habit. We believe drinking sodas is a bad habit.

But these are not the kinds of opinions that we are striving for in our evaluations. Sophisticated writers don't settle for saying things are merely "good" or "bad," or that they "like" or "dislike" them. Instead writers should offer an evaluation that is more specific based on the results of their research.

Take, for example, the malaria vaccine that I have been researching. Here is the initial opinion I wrote down in my pre-writing exercise:

> I think that giving children in Africa a malaria vaccine is a wonderful idea since it will probably save many lives.

After doing my research, I still believe it is a good idea to vaccinate children in Africa against malaria, and I found hard evidence to prove that it will save lives. However, during my research I also realized that most people would probably agree with this opinion statement. I wouldn't need to convince them with evidence.

What about this opinion statement?

> It is promising that researchers seem to have finally developed an effective malaria vaccine. However, a vaccine cannot stop malaria altogether, so I believe proven methods for preventing malaria – such as distributing mosquito nets – need to be a higher priority.

Or this one?

> Recent strides in developing a vaccine reveal that we may soon be able to greatly decrease the number of deaths from malaria, but I think it is also important to pursue other preventative methods since a vaccine will only protect children.

See how much more specific these statements are. They communicate that I "like" the idea of a malaria vaccine, but they don't stop there. They also communicate that no matter how much anyone "likes" the idea of a vaccine, it doesn't change the reality that malaria will continue to be a problem.

CWJ

In this capsule, we learned that summaries provide the necessary background for opinion statements. Why don't you give both a try?

1. Think about your summary as the "recap" that brings the audience up-to-speed before the upcoming attraction. What pieces of background information do your readers need to know about the event to follow along with your evaluation? Sketch a series of three to five simple images that represent the background facts of your event. Write a one sentence caption for each picture.

2. Return to your pre-writing exercise from 3.2.3. You should have written your initial opinion of the event there. What was it? How has your understanding of the event changed through conducting research? Write down what you have learned through your research.

3. Now try your hand at writing an opinion statement. Compose two or three versions of a revised opinion statement. Put a star next to the statement you believe (1) most accurately expresses your evaluation of the event and (2) can be supported with the source information you have.

(Remember that your evaluation doesn't need to change completely from your initial opinion. However, it should become more focused and specific. You know more now than you did before conducting research, so your evaluation of the current event should reflect your new knowledge.)

CAPSULE 5 3.2.5

GETTING TO THE WHY: REASONS AND EVIDENCE

Constructing a focused opinion statement should make the rest of your evaluation easier. Why? Well, you have conducted a lot of research, and you have quite a bit of information at your fingertips. But now you don't have to worry about including all of the interesting research you found. You only need to include information that offers support for your specific opinion.

But how do you organize this information? Most writers organize their evaluative arguments according to reasons. Reasons answer the question, "Why do I hold this opinion?"

The writer of the school garden article offers reasons to support her opinion that students and parents should give the idea of a learning garden a chance. Return to 3.2.2 and use a highlighter to mark the reasons the writer includes.

What did you come up with? I found three reasons:

▶ The idea of creating a school garden is not new.
▶ School gardens have benefits outside the classroom.
▶ There are ways to minimize the costs of building and maintaining the garden.

Writers don't only offer reasons to support their opinions. They construct an additional layer of support for their arguments by providing evidence to explain their reasons. Evidence is more specific than reasons and may include statistics or quotes from involved parties. For this reason, evidence needs to be attributed to a source.

Using a different color highlighter, mark the evidence the writer offers to explain her reasons. There should be more than one piece of evidence to support each reason. Here are just a few of the ones she incorporates. See if you can identify them all.

▶ School gardens can be found from Hawaii to Maine and from preschools to high schools.
▶ These gardens introduce students to new food sources.
▶ Local gardeners can volunteer their time to help offset the costs of tending the garden.

As you identified the evidence, did you notice any evidence based on the writer's own experience? What was it? How did her use of personal experience influence your response to her argument?

Although we have focused on finding evidence in sources throughout this lesson, we do want to emphasize that your own experiences can also serve as evidence in your evaluations. If you have a personal knowledge of the subject you are writing about, incorporating it within your evaluation can be a very effective tactic. Doing so can enhance your **rapport** with readers who may become more convinced of your genuine investment in the subject and thus more disposed to trust your judgment. So, don't shy away from incorporating personal experiences when they apply.

THE PROFESSOR'S OFFICE

There is a common misconception about writers that I tend to hear from students. It is best depicted through the image of the hermit writer who has locked himself in a room away from the world to write whatever his fancy suggests. This popular image suggests that we somehow view writers as separate from the world, almost indifferent to it, because they choose to inhabit a world of their own imagination. Movies, television, and even books have all contributed to the construction of this image.

However, it is more often the case that writers write in response to the world. It is the events of this life that inspire them to write, that may even make it impossible for them to keep from writing.

One of the most influential American writers in history, Ralph Waldo Emerson, offered evaluations of nineteenth-century society in his essays. He challenged the members of the young nation to create a uniquely American society, rather than simply following Europe's example. He was also critical of slavery in the years before the Civil War and used his lecturing and writing to influence others in favor of abolition.

In this century, the controversial author Ayaan Hirsi Ali has become a **zealous** *advocate for women. She has utilized the pen to draw attention to civil rights violations against women in Muslim countries. In her autobiography, she describes instances of great cruelty she experienced and witnessed during her childhood. These stories serve as evidence to support her argument that women and girls throughout the world need to receive protection from abuse and injustice.*

Neither of these writers separated themselves from society and its issues in order to write. Instead they engaged the relevant issues of their day, adding their voice and opinions to the conversation.

As writers, we can also join the conversation going on in the world around us. So even if you prefer to write in your room with your door closed, in order to maintain your relevance as a writer, it's important to come out every once in awhile and take a look around. You might find something that angers, excites, or saddens you. And you might find that you have something important to say about it.

CWJ

IN YOUR JOURNAL ▶

Constructing a well-researched, fair evaluation of a current event that is going on in your world is one way to contribute to the conversation. You have already formulated an opinion about your current event. All you have to do now is support it.

1. Ask yourself, "Why do I hold this opinion?" Identify three or four reasons why you feel this way. Write your reasons in complete sentences in your CWJ, leaving space between them for evidence.

2. Now look back through the answers to your criteria questions in 3.2.3, and read back through your highlighted sources to find specific evidence for each of your reasons. This is a good place to incorporate statistics and quotes from people involved in the event. Your personal experience can be relevant here too. Try to identify more than one piece of evidence for each reason. Organize your evidence by writing it down beneath the reason it supports, and make sure you give credit to your sources!

3. As the professor suggested, effective writers engage the issues of their society. They write about things that are meaningful to them. Both Emerson and Ali saw injustice happening in their world and used the written word to influence others, to offer an alternative.

Though you may not be writing about injustice, as a writer you should always consider how the event you are evaluating is relevant to your life. Spend some time answering the following questions in your CWJ:

▶ Does this event affect you directly or indirectly? Does it affect anyone you know or a group of people you care about? How so?

▶ Why do you think it is important to write about this event? Or what do you hope to accomplish through writing about this event?

At this point you have successfully completed all of the components of an evaluation. You have researched, formulated an opinion, identified reasons and evidence to support that opinion, and considered the overarching importance of what you are writing about. Congratulations!

THE RIGHT WORD

 It's time to hunt for synonyms once again. Here are the five vocabulary words you learned in this lesson in context. Replace the word in bold with the synonym that best expresses its meaning.

1. The result might be the **affirmation** of some truth, or might be the denial of some falsehood.
2. You may be surprised, as I was, to hear that there is a **precedent** for these gardens at other schools in the nation.
3. Principal Parker, one of the garden's most vocal **proponents**, argues that a school garden will have benefits beyond the classroom.
4. Doing so can enhance your **rapport** with readers who may become more convinced of your genuine investment in the subject and thus more disposed to trust your judgment.
5. In this century, the controversial author Ayaan Hirsi Ali has become a **zealous** advocate for women.

Write with WORLD

UNIT 3 / LESSON 3

REVIEWING TEXTS

REPORTING ON A BOOK

CAPSULE 1

3.3.1

WHAT'S IT ALL ABOUT: SUMMARIZING YOUR BOOK

When you finish the last page of a book you have been reading, what do you do next? Fall asleep because you stayed up way too late to find out what was going to happen? Cry, yell, laugh, or throw the book across the room depending on how it ended? Reach for the television remote since you were required to finish reading before you could watch your favorite show?

If you really liked – or really didn't like – the book, you may be inclined to talk to someone about it. You might call a friend to tell her she must borrow this book. Or you might complain to your parents that reading the book was a total waste of time.

Over the next few days you may find yourself thinking about the book at times, reliving the plot, revisiting the characters, or rethinking the ending in your head.

In each of these instances – whether you are sharing your thoughts with others or silently contemplating a book's merit – you are evaluating what you have read.

When you take the next step and translate these thoughts into writing, you create a book review. A book review, the genre that concerns us in this lesson, is simply a written evaluation of a book by someone who has read and considered it.

There are two basic components of a book review:

1.   A concise summary of the book
2.   A critical assessment (analysis) of the book

Read this passage about Charles Dickens' *A Tale of Two Cities*. Pay attention to whether or not it contains the two components necessary for a book review.

◄ IN YOUR JOURNAL

A Tale of Two Cities is a historical novel written by the famous Victorian author Charles Dickens. It holds distinction as one of the most famous works of fiction ever written. Over a century and a half after its publication, it is still required reading at most high schools in the nation.

As was the custom in 1859 when the novel was published, the book was released in the form of weekly installments in a magazine. It took seven months and 31 installments to issue the entire story, after which Dickens published the novel in book form.

Dickens' tale begins in 1775 when France is becoming more and more unstable on the road to revolution. The Frenchman, Dr. Manette, has just been released from an eighteen-year-long unjust imprisonment in the Bastille. His angelic daughter, Lucie, nurses him back to health in England. Sydney Carton and Charles Darnay – who incidentally look very much alike – both fall in love with Lucie.

Lucie chooses to marry Charles and start a family, but her husband's secret identity as a French nobleman threatens to ruin their happiness. When it is discovered that Charles' father, the Marquis, was responsible for Dr. Manette's imprisonment, Charles is required to pay for the sins of his father. He is imprisoned in the Bastille and condemned to the guillotine. All hope seems lost.

It is at this point that Sydney's love for Lucie causes him to step in and finally become a better man by sacrificing his own life. The final sentence of the text, spoken by Sydney, tops the charts as one of the best last lines in novel history: "It is a far, far better thing that I do, than I have ever done; it is a far, far better rest that I go to than I have ever known."

This passage definitely covers the first component of a book review by providing a useful description of Dickens' novel. It offers us:

▶ Background on the author and the text
▶ Information about the book's popularity over time
▶ A description of the book's basic plot

However, the summary is not necessarily concise and it should have a spoiler alert at the beginning. It offers a bit too much information, uncovering some of the plot twists that readers would want to discover on their own. Remember that your job as a reviewer is to give readers enough background to help them follow your review. You don't want to tell them so much that they don't need to read the book for themselves!

Does the writer include the second component of a book review by providing his assessment of the text? In other words, can you determine the writer's opinion of *A Tale of Two Cities* based on this passage? Do you think he would recommend reading this book?

It's hard to tell. Nowhere does the writer offer his opinion of the text. He does include a generalized opinion of the book by talking about its popularity with readers, but this too is factual. His comments are informative rather than evaluative. (In fact, the writer could have written this passage based on a basic knowledge of the book, without even reading it at all.)

The kind of objective reporting on a book this writer engages in can be very useful to readers. Think about the audience for a library catalog or bookstore's website. These readers may appreciate a summary to help them identify a book, but would rather not be influenced by another person's opinion of the book.

In general, however, the audience of a book review hopes to learn something more than just basic information. They expect to read a critique of the book as well.

Granted, it is daunting to think about reviewing a book, especially one as famous as *A Tale of Two Cities*. You may be wondering, "What could I possibly have to contribute?" But remember that your opinion as a reader is valid, even if you aren't an expert. Anyone who can read a book, express their opinion on it, and back that opinion up with evidence can write an effective book review.

CWJ

In the remainder of this lesson, we will be walking you through the process of composing a book review, so let's start with the obvious first step: picking a book.

◀ IN YOUR JOURNAL

If you have just completed a book and it is fresh on your mind, it might be a good choice. A favorite book that you have read many times could be a good choice too. Any book will work as long as (1) it is at or above your reading level (no picture books, please) and (2) you have something to say about it.

Once you have selected your book, you will want to take some time to reacquaint yourself with it. Skim back through, reminding yourself of character names and plot details. If you took notes while you were reading the book, pull those out and take a look at them.

Answer these questions about your book in your CWJ:

1.   What is the book's title and genre? Is it a novel, biography, play?
2.   Who is the author? Do you know anything interesting about the author? For instance, is this author **prolific** or is this his first book?
3.   When was the book originally published? Many books have multiple editions, so look for the earliest publication date you can find.
4.   How has the book been received by audiences? Has it won any awards or earned distinction as a "bestseller?" Or is it relatively unknown?
5.   Write a one to two paragraph summary of the book. Your summary should answer the question, "What is this book about?"
   a.   If you are reviewing a fictional work like a novel write down who the significant characters are and their roles in the text, as well as a brief summary of what happens in the book.

b.   If you are reviewing a work of nonfiction such as a book of essays, try to explain the author's argument, or what he is trying to prove to readers. What techniques does he use (research, statistics, personal stories, etc.) to make his point?

CAPSULE 2 3.3.2

BE A CRITIC, NOT JUST CRITICAL

Take a look at another sample review written about Dickens' classic novel. How does it compare with the one you read in 3.3.1?

A Tale of Two Cities by Charles Dickens is an extremely long book – and a total bore. I recommend that you save yourself the trouble and avoid this one.

Why did I dislike this book so much?

First, there were so many characters that I couldn't keep up with them all. What's the point of including a character if your readers can't remember him halfway through the book?

The language used in the text proved difficult to wade through as well. I'm not sure the author knows how to write dialogue because the characters' interactions came across as stiff and overly formal. As I read, all I could think was, "That's not how people talk in real life."

And finally, after suffering through forty-five chapters, the least Dickens could have done is offer us a happy ending. But this book is extremely sad. I mean cry-yourself-to-sleep-for-a-week depressing.

In conclusion, if you are looking for interesting, worthwhile reading, try the dictionary instead.

Unlike the previous example, this review offers lots of opinions about the book.

First, let's consider the positives. The passage is clearly arranged with the writer addressing a specific aspect of the text in each paragraph.

Furthermore, we know exactly how the writer feels about *A Tale of Two Cities* and can be certain that she would not recommend it! In that sense, the passage somewhat fulfills the second component of a book review: a critical assessment of the book.

The problem is that this writer's version of a "critical" assessment is not the version readers of a book review are looking for. This review is critical in one sense of the word. It is negative and overly judgmental. However, the kind of critical assessment a book reviewer should strive for is one that provides a careful evaluation, not just a list of complaints.

A book reviewer is a critic, not just critical!

Another problem with this passage is that the writer fails to offer us a summary of the book, so her evaluation takes place outside of context. For example, she complains of the language being difficult to follow, but if she had mentioned that the book was published in England in 1859, that would explain why the language seems stiff and formal. People spoke and wrote differently then.

And even if she didn't care for the sad ending, the setting of the French Revolution and the themes of self-sacrifice and redemption could have at least explained the ending better. In fact, viewed in this context, the ending might be viewed as hopeful, rather than depressing.

The writer's assessments are not necessarily wrong. It's perfectly acceptable for a writer to find fault with a book. A review need not be glowing. It just needs to be balanced and fair. But because this writer doesn't tell us what the book is supposed to be about, we can't necessarily trust – or even understand – her judgments.

A clear summary of the book's content and specific examples from the text are necessary to provide a solid foundation for your critique.

WORLD WISDOM

WORLD Magazine writer Susan Olasky is no stranger to reviewing books. Here she provides some helpful guidelines for getting started.

Before you can write a good book review you need to find a book that is worth reviewing. If the book doesn't fascinate, delight, or challenge you, it's probably not worth writing about. If the book is ho hum, so will be your review.

Once you've found a book, you need to read it carefully so that you can summarize its plot or argument. You need to answer the question, what is the book about? You don't need to spell out every plot twist because then people won't read the book.

You also need to let the reader know what the author thinks about his subject. Does the author of a book about UFOs, for instance, believe that space aliens live in his garage? Sometimes it's harder to figure this out with fiction. An author who writes a story about talking animals probably doesn't believe that talking animals exist. But even in a fantasy story, the author is creating a world. What kind of world is it?

Last, you need to let the reader know what you think about the book. Here are some questions to help you: How does the Bible help you think about the author's ideas or the story? What kinds of choices do the characters have to make? With what are they struggling? Does the author resolve those issues in a satisfying way? Does the book have a sense of right and wrong? Are you encouraged to root for those things that are good, true, and beautiful—or do you find yourself rooting for something that isn't good? Is the book well-written? Does it have objectionable elements?

CWJ

IN YOUR JOURNAL ▶

Take some time to consider your book in the context of Mrs. Olasky's comments. Is the book you have chosen a book worth reviewing? If it is, try to explain in writing why it is worth reviewing. If you determine it isn't, go ahead and select a different book now.

We focused on summarizing the contents of the book in your last CWJ entry. Now it's time to tell readers what you think about the book. Sometimes you may have a "feeling" about a book, but it's hard to explain why you feel that way.

Here, again, are Mrs. Olasky's questions – as well as a few extra – to help you put your feelings about the book into words.

1. What three adjectives would you use to describe this book? Why did you pick these adjectives?
2. What (if anything) did you learn from reading this book?
3. Does reading this book make you want to read other books by the author? Why or why not?
4. What is the most interesting part of the book? The least interesting?
5. How does the Bible help you think about the author's ideas or the story?
6. What kinds of choices do the characters have to make? With what are they struggling? Does the author resolve the characters' issues in a satisfying way?
7. Does the book have a sense of right and wrong?
8. Are you encouraged to root for those things that are good, true, and beautiful—or do you find yourself rooting for something that isn't good?
9. Is the book well-written? If so, copy a favorite sentence or two from the text. If it's poorly written, write down an example of that instead.
10. Does it have objectionable elements? What are they? What types of readers would be bothered by them?

As you answer these questions, make sure to offer specific examples from the book to explain why you feel this way. Write down the page number each example is on so that you can find it easily when it comes time to write your review.

CAPSULE 3

STRIKING THE RIGHT BALANCE: SUMMARIZE THEN ANALYZE

Hopefully you have figured out that an effective book review needs to offer (1) an appropriate amount of background information and (2) a fair evaluation of the book's strengths and weaknesses.

See if this final review of *A Tale of Two Cities* gets it right.

A Tale of Two Cities, a historical novel written by the famous Victorian author Charles Dickens, holds distinction as one of the most famous works of fiction ever written. Its continued popularity is revealed in that it is still required reading for most high schoolers in the nation. In fact, I recently read it in my English course. Although the text may be difficult for a twenty-first century audience of teenagers to fully appreciate, it remains an exciting and spiritually instructive text for yet another generation of Christian readers.

*The tale begins in 1775 when France's political and social stability is crumbling on the road to revolution. The Frenchman, Dr. Manette, has been released from an eighteen-year-long unjust imprisonment in the Bastille due to the corruption of the ruling classes. His angelic daughter, Lucie, who nurses him back to health in England, is being pursued by look-a-like suitors: the **hedonistic** Sydney Carton and the virtuous Charles Darnay. This text is so full of surprises that I must avoid giving away too much. I will just say that as the plot develops, the fates of Lucie's two admirers become inextricably connected. Ultimately, Dickens uses this relationship to consider whether someone like Sydney, who has lived life solely for his own pleasure, is capable of self-sacrifice.*

*Dickens' style, which is full of long, colorful descriptions and an extensive cast of characters, can be somewhat overwhelming. Our current generation of "texters" may find fault with this aspect of the text since we privilege **brevity** – think LOL, OMW, IMHO – in our daily writing. People who enjoy a clean, modern style of writing won't fall in love with Dickens' flowery, sometimes convoluted prose. The opening sentence boasting over 100 words may be enough to turn some readers away.*

However, when one considers when and how A Tale of Two Cities *was originally published, it is easier to appreciate the style. Nineteenth-century readers actually read the text in weekly installments in a literary magazine, so they spent seven months digesting only one or two chapters at a time. I wonder if today's readers would enjoy this text more if we read only a chapter a week, giving ourselves more time to get to know the characters and consider the events as Dickens intended. Of course, this would be nearly impossible to accomplish in a normal school setting, but it could be done as part of a summer reading program.*

Because Dickens wanted to keep readers interested from week to week, he filled the text with cliffhangers and plot twists. Even today these elements are just as surprising and welcome to readers as they probably were to the original audience. For example, you will be shocked to find out who Charles' father is and the nature of his crimes. It is like something out of a movie! This element of surprise is part of what made nineteenth-century readers stay tuned every week and also makes the text unexpectedly riveting to a present-day audience.

The ending of the text is heartbreaking, but in the midst of sadness, there is also hope. In 1 Timothy 1:15, Paul says that Christ came to save all sinners, of whom he calls himself the chief. Dickens' story is consistent with the scriptures for he shows that even the worst of sinners can be redeemed. When the text ends with one of the most famous final lines in literature, "It is a far, far better thing that I do, than I have ever done; it is a far, far better rest that I go to than I have ever known," we know that hope is still alive.

Is this text still intriguing and relevant today, especially to a Christian readership? Absolutely. Will a sixteen- or seventeen-year-old be able to fully appreciate what it has to offer despite its outdated manner of writing? I'm not sure. Does this mean teachers should replace this classic with a more recent, less challenging text? Absolutely not. Dickens may be a challenging read, but the truths that students will find are undoubtedly worth the effort it takes to uncover them.

After reading this review, what is your reaction?

Do you feel as if you received too much, too little, or adequate background information about the text to understand the writer's commentary? Look back through the review and circle the passage where the writer summarizes the text.

This review offers a much fuller summary than the example in 3.3.2, but avoids the pitfall of spoiling the story by revealing too many plot details as did the example in 3.3.1. Overall it does a commendable job condensing forty-five chapters of story into a single paragraph! She even explains what may have been one of Dickens' purposes in crafting this narrative when she concludes, *"Ultimately, Dickens uses this relationship to consider whether someone like Sydney, who has lived life solely for his own pleasure, is capable of self-sacrifice."*

Now for the second requirement of a book review: Did you get a clear sense of what the reviewer thinks about the book? Return to the passage and highlight where the writer states her overall opinion of the text.

Where did you find it? I identified a specific evaluation of *A Tale of Two Cities* at the end of the first paragraph. (She also could have waited until after she summarized the text to do so, but putting her opinion close to the beginning helps give readers a sense of where the review is heading early on.) She writes, *"Although the text may be difficult for a twenty-first century audience of teenagers to fully appreciate, it remains an exciting and spiritually instructive text for yet another generation of Christian readers."*

What element(s) of the text does the writer identify as most effective? What element(s) of the text does the writer identify as less effective? Write "effective" or "ineffective" in the margin to indicate where these elements are addressed.

As you can see, this writer's opinion isn't completely positive or completely negative. Instead, she offers a balanced assessment based on her personal experience reading the text. Additional information about how and when the book was published also help her have a better understanding of the book than the reviewer in 3.3.2. We can see that she has done some research to be a better reviewer.

You're probably relieved to see that this review writer didn't deal with every aspect of the text. No one has time for that, especially with a book written by Charles Dickens! Instead, she focused on the aspects she thought would help her audience determine if this text is a worthwhile read.

So remember: The purpose of your book review is to be helpful to your audience, not just to complete an assignment by praising or complaining about a book.

We'll talk more about how you can target your remarks to a specific audience in the next capsule. But first…

CWJ

Before you sit down to compose your book review, we would like you to spend some time reading reviews by other writers. Doing so will offer you a fuller understanding of the genre. It will also help you identify what makes a book review more or less successful – and hopefully introduce you to some techniques you can incorporate into your own writing.

◄ IN YOUR JOURNAL

The Internet is a great resource for finding book reviews. If you have a specific book you want to read a review of, simply type the title of the book, followed by the words "book review," into your search engine and see what comes up. (You may want to search for reviews of the book you are planning to review in order to get a sense of what others have to say about it. Just be careful to avoid copying any of the ideas and opinions you may find.)

We encourage you to read through at least three or four different reviews to find the one you want to analyze. Once you have chosen a review that looks promising, answer these questions in your CWJ:

1.   What is the title and author of the book being reviewed?
2.   What, if any, additional information does the book review writer offer about the author or the book (awards the book or its author has won, publication information, public opinion about the book, other books by the same author)?

3. How much time/space does the writer spend summarizing the book's contents? Does the writer offer an adequate summary of the text in order for you to follow the book review?

4. Does the writer offer his evaluation of the book? If so, where did you find his opinion and what is it?

5. What information does the writer use to support his opinion?

6. Who is the book reviewer? (teenager, parent, professional author, librarian)

7. Who do you think is the audience for this review? (Consider what kind of website the review is posted on.)

8. How would you describe the writer's style? For example, are the sentences and paragraphs short or long? Is the language he uses formal or informal (sophisticated vocabulary or slang)? Does the writer maintain a serious tone or does he incorporate humor?

9. On a scale of one (not at all) to five (very), how successful do you think the book review was? Explain your rating.

CAPSULE 4 3.3.4

DIFFERENCE OF OPINION: TARGETING YOUR REVIEW TO A SPECIFIC AUDIENCE

Now that you have analyzed a review on your own, we think you are ready to work on composing your own book review.

But where should you start? When you review a book there are a lot of elements you could discuss. However, if you know who your readers are, you can tailor your review to their interests or needs.

First think about the review of *A Tale of Two Cities* from 3.3.3. What audience do you think this writer is addressing? As you read back through the review, circle any possible audiences the writer mentions.

A few descriptors caught my eye: high schoolers, teachers, Christian readers. But how do you know which of these groups is the specific audience?

Well the writer mentions she has just read the book as a school requirement and is a member of the texting generation so she would appear to be a high school student. Does it sound like she is writing to an audience of other high schoolers?

No, not really. The language used in this review is more formal and the vocabulary more advanced than one might expect from a student who is writing to other students. Since she argues that the book should remain required reading in schools, it is likely she is writing for someone with the authority to make that choice, probably a teacher or administrator. Furthermore, her focus on Christian elements within the book suggests she is probably writing to teachers or administrators at a private Christian school.

Now look at the book review you analyzed for your CWJ exercise in 3.3.3. What audience did you identify for this review? What aspects of the review (word choice, length, level of formality, the website it was published on) gave you clues about who the review was written for?

Why is identifying a specific audience for your book review so important?

To answer that question, let's turn to Aristotle for a moment. You've probably heard of this Greek philosopher who was a student of Plato. In Rhetoric, Aristotle identifies three interconnected elements to any writing situation:

▶ Writer
▶ Subject
▶ Audience

But what does this mean? Well, Aristotle says that constructing an argument isn't just about the writer and his subject. It's also about who the writer is writing to. And you can't create an effective argument without taking your readers into account.

For example, your relationship with your readers is an important factor. Are they friends, family, or authority figures? Is the audience friendly or hostile? You also want to consider how much they know about the subject. If you are writing about smart phones to an audience of grandparents you will probably need to explain more than if you are writing to your classmates.

Ultimately Aristotle tells us that when we think about who our readers are and what they may or may not know, we increase the effectiveness of our words.

So let's see how this philosophy will help us with our book reviews.

Here's an example. If I were reviewing *The Call of the Wild* by Jack London for my son's Boy Scout troop, I would offer a different overall opinion than if I were reviewing it for the members of his grandmother's book club.

Can you tell which opinion statement is meant for which audience?

▶ Don't let the fact that it was written in 1903 fool you. Jack London's *The Call of the Wild* boasts just as much violence, adventure, and heroism as any video game you can play.
▶ *The Call of the Wild* would be the perfect book to read alongside your grandson or recommend to your adventure-loving husband; however, this "survival of the fittest" tale may not be as relevant to adult female readers.

I'm sure it wasn't too hard to tell which statement fit which audience. The first statement uses informal language and compares the book to video games, something Boy Scouts would probably be familiar with.

The second statement is longer, more formal, and actually refers to an audience of "adult female readers."

Notice that I recommend *The Call of the Wild* to the Boy Scouts, but tell the book club ladies that this might not be the best choice for them. Does this mean that my opinion of the book changed?

Not at all. It just shows that I am considering my readers and tailoring my recommendations to their age and interests.

Your turn. Try writing an opinion statement about your chosen book for two different audiences. You can use the sample audiences we did – a Boy Scout troop and your grandmother's book club – or you can choose two audiences that make more sense for your particular text.

How did writing for a specific audience change the way you presented your opinion?

If you haven't already, go ahead and select an audience for your book review (a sibling or cousin, the church youth choir, readers of your blog, your grandparents, the principal of your school, etc.). Now write an opinion statement for that specific audience to include in your review.

STYLE TIME: PICKING THE PERFECT TENSE

i Here are the verb tenses you have to choose from when you write:

Present Tenses:
Present – Graham *walks* his dog every day.
Present Perfect – Graham *has walked* his dog many times.
Present Progressive – Graham *is walking* his dog right now.
Present Perfect Progressive – Graham *has been walking* his dog since he was eight.

Past Tenses:
Past – Graham *walked* his dog last night.
Past Perfect – Graham *had walked* his dog all the way down the block before he heard his mom calling for him to return.
Past Progressive – Graham *was walking* his dog when he found a lost kitten.
Past Perfect Progressive – Graham *had been walking* his dog for five minutes before he realized it wasn't actually his dog.

Future Tenses:
Future – Graham *will walk* his dog this afternoon.
Future Perfect – Graham *will have walked* his dog only five times this week.
Future Progressive – Graham *will be walking* his dog when his father gets home from work.
Future Perfect Progressive – Graham *will have been walking* his dog for half his life by the time he is sixteen.

If you are like most people, you probably had no idea there were this many verb tenses! But don't be alarmed. There are only three basic time frames for your writing: present, past, and future.

The number one rule with verb tense is:

BE CONSISTENT!

Avoid shifting from one tense to another in the middle of a sentence, paragraph, or essay.

Inconsistent:
I *ran* a competitive race, but Oliver *will win* because he runs faster.

Consistent:
I *ran* a competitive race, but Oliver *won* because he ran faster.

The original sentence begins in the present tense but gets confusing when it shifts to future tense in the middle and present tense at the end. The second sentence is preferable because it remains in past tense from beginning to end.

Inconsistent:
Everyone *had been staring* while Oscar *devours* twenty packets of ketchup.

Consistent:
Everyone *stares* while Oscar *devours* twenty packets of ketchup.

The second sentence is better because it remains in the present tense. Both actions – Oscar devouring and everyone staring – take place concurrently, or at the same time, so they should be in the same tense.

Is there ever a reason to shift tenses within a sentence? YES.

It's okay to change tenses when you need to show that the actions within a sentence occurred at different times.

Consistent but Incorrect:
Although this book *was published* in the nineteenth century, it *remained* a bestseller even today.

Inconsistent but Correct:
Although this book *was published* in the nineteenth century, it *remains* a bestseller even today.

In this example, the time frames – the nineteenth century and today – are clearly different. Therefore, different tenses are required.

Future tense is often mixed with the present tense, as in the following example. (Future is not usually combined with the past tense.)

Consistent but Incorrect:
If he *feels* better, Henry *returns* to school tomorrow.

Inconsistent but Correct:
If he *feels* better, Henry *will return* to school tomorrow.

Think logically about what you are trying to communicate, and the choice of tense will probably be obvious.

Activity: Most of the writing you will be doing calls for the use of present tense. Return to the book review in 3.3.1 and highlight the verbs, making a note whenever the tense shifts out of the present. Why did it shift?

As you work on your book review, check your verbs to make sure you remain in the present tense throughout. Remember, it's okay to shift tenses at certain times, such as when you are talking about a deceased author or predicting a book's future success. But always return to present tense immediately after.

CWJ

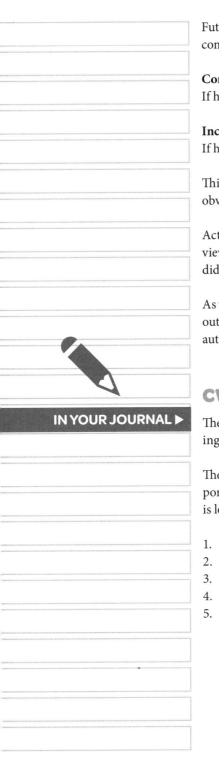

IN YOUR JOURNAL ▶

The time has arrived to write your book review. At this point, you already have a lot of the work of reviewing your book done. You can find this work in your CWJ as indicated below.

These are the elements you will want to include in your review with a suggestion for about how long each portion should be. You may want to use sticky notes to flag the pages in your CWJ where this information is located. This will make it easier to flip back and forth between them as you write.

1. Introduction of the book and its author – one paragraph [3.3.1]
2. Summary of the book's contents – one to two paragraphs [3.3.1]
3. Opinion statement – one to two sentences [3.3.4]
4. Critical assessment of the book – two to four paragraphs [3.3.2]
5. Conclusion with your recommendation for readers – one short paragraph

WRITING A BOOK REVIEW WITH STYLE

THE PROFESSOR'S OFFICE

Personal style. It's a part of who you are.

Style shows itself in the clothes you wear. Maybe you like to dress in a casual fashion with untucked t-shirts and comfortable jeans. Or maybe you prefer a more polished look with a matching belt and shoes, hair meticulously styled, and clothes free from holes and stains.

Style shows itself in the music you listen to. Do you enjoy the challenge of classical compositions, the twang of country western artists, or the catchy rhythm of pop music?

*Style also shows itself in how you write. All writers have a personal style. And the best writers become **synonymous** with that style.*

Authors such as Virginia Woolf, William Faulkner, and James Joyce are known for a style of writing called stream-of-consciousness that is meant to resemble people's thoughts. The opening lines of A Portrait of an Artist as a Young Man *(1914-15), in which that author tries to mimic the thoughts of a little boy, have come to represent this particular style.*

> Once upon a time and a very good time it was there was a moocow coming down along the road and this moocow that was coming down along the road met a nicens little boy named baby tuckoo...
>
> His father told him that story: his father looked at him through a glass: he had a hairy face. He was baby tuckoo. The moocow came down the road where Betty Burne lived: she sold lemon platt.

Willa Cather and Bret Harte are associated with styles of writing that incorporate the unrefined dialects of people such as immigrants and coal miners. In this passage from Cather's My Ántonia *(1918), the title character explains in broken English that her father misses life in their homeland of Bohemia.*

> My papa sad for the old country. He not look good. He never make music any more. At home he play violin all the time; for weddings and for dance. Here never. When I beg him for play, he shake his head no. Some days he take his violin out of his box and make with his fingers on the strings, like this, but never he make the music. He don't like this kawn-tree.

Jonathan Swift and Mark Twain are writers who are known for using a form of humor known as satire to critique the society in which they lived. You may be familiar with Swift's famous work, A Modest Proposal

(1729), in which he suggests that Irish children be sold as food to deal with the nation's poverty. Here Swift seems as if he is trying to make his plan sound appealing, but he is actually being **satirical***, or showing how absurd it really is.*

> *I have been assured by a very knowing American of my acquaintance in London, that a young healthy child well nursed is at a year old a most delicious, nourishing, and wholesome food, whether stewed, roasted, baked, or boiled; and I make no doubt that it will equally serve in a fricassee or a ragout.*

All of these writers wrote in very different styles, and each was very successful.

Part of your success as a writer is dependent on identifying and honing your personal writing style.

That's why I encourage my students to read A LOT. And to read LOTS of different authors. As you read, you will start to pick out styles of writing that speak to you. Then you can "try on" those styles in writing until you find the right fit.

Are you known for being funny? If so, incorporate humor and wit in your writing.

Do you enjoy writing long, flowing sentences with lots of description? Then put your skills of elaboration to work and paint a picture in words.

Maybe you prefer a streamlined style that's more to-the-point? Use active verbs and short paragraphs to keep your readers moving.

Don't know what you like? Then try them all. Let others read your work and ask for their opinions. When you find the one that fits, you will know.

As the professor notes, part of your success as a writer is dependent upon your ability to establish a unique, personal writing style. But that is not all there is to style.

Style is also influenced by the medium in which you are writing. Medium is another word for the means you use to communicate your ideas. Newspapers, magazines, published books, blogs, handwritten letters, e-mails, and text messages are all examples of different written mediums.

The style a writer uses is often dependent on his chosen medium. For instance, if I were writing a letter to my grandmother, my style would be much more informal, personal, and even affectionate than if I were writing a newspaper article. Newspapers have strict word limits so writers need to get to the facts quickly and make their point with clear, no-nonsense wording.

Today many people use e-book readers and smart phones to do their reading. The small screens on these devices make it difficult to digest a lot of material at once, so these mediums require a concise style of writing.

This review of Meir Shalev's *My Russian Grandmother and Her American Vacuum Cleaner: A Family Memoir* by Susan Olasky is posted on the *WORLD on Campus* website. It illustrates how one book review writer adapts her style to suit currently popular digital mediums. Olasky writes,

> *This rambling family memoir by Israeli novelist Meir Shalev shows how perspective changes everything. At the heart of the memoir is Grandma Tonia. She could be depicted as a bitter complainer, whose habits of cleanliness drove her family crazy. Instead, Shalev portrays her as the tenacious matriarch of a close-knit family. Her mangled figures of speech and her never-ending battle against dirt become the grist of family stories that hold the family together. Shalev's memoir won't appeal to those who want straight and to-the-point stories, but he will delight those who appreciate the leisurely unfolding of funny family tales during a pioneering period in Nahalal, a rural farm community in northern Israel.*

Did you notice how efficiently Mrs. Olasky fulfills all the elements of a book review in a short paragraph? I could easily pull up this review on my smart phone at the book store and get enough information to decide if I want to purchase this book.

What we want you to understand through this example and the Professor's Office is that writers make several stylistic choices when they write. They write according to their personal style and what type of style is best suited to the medium in which they are writing.

Since you already have a rough draft of your book review written, in this capsule we want you to spend some time focusing on and fine tuning your style.

◀ IN YOUR JOURNAL

CWJ

In 3.3.4 we asked you to select a specific audience for your review. Now ask yourself, "What is an effective medium I can use to reach this audience?"

1. Select a specific medium for your review. Here are a few you can pick from or you can think of your own:

   ▶ Handwritten letter or e-mail (to friend or family member)
   ▶ Personal blog entry
   ▶ Article for school newspaper or church newsletter
   ▶ Formal typed letter (to principal, teacher, or other authority figure)
   ▶ Short blurb for a website hosting book reviews (think Amazon.com)

2.   In your CWJ, brainstorm a list of the conventions, or the usual features, of the medium you have chosen. For example, the conventions of a blog entry might include:

▶   Catchy headline to grab readers' interest
▶   Short paragraphs
▶   Conversational language (may even include "texting talk" to engage youthful readers)
▶   Invitation for readers to comment on the blog entry with their own opinions
▶   Links to other websites where readers can find additional information or a different opinion
▶   Personal information such as the music you were listening to as you wrote or the mood you were in *if it helps explain your approach to the subject*

3.   Revise your book review by rewriting it according to the conventions of your chosen medium. Try to incorporate aspects of your personal writing style if it fits the medium.

4.   How did writing in a different medium change your review?

THE RIGHT WORD

 You've digested five new vocabulary words in this lesson. You should have already defined them in your CWJ, so it's time to grab your thesaurus and find an acceptable replacement for each one. Here are the words once again:

1.   For instance, is this author **prolific** or is this his first book?
2.   His angelic daughter, Lucie, who nurses him back to health in England, is being pursued by look-a-like suitors: the **hedonistic** Sydney Carton and the virtuous Charles Darnay.
3.   Our current generation of "texters" may find fault with this aspect of the text since we privilege **brevity** – think LOL, OMW, IMHO – in our daily writing.
4.   And the best writers become **synonymous** with that style.
5.   Here Swift seems as if he is trying to make his plan sound appealing, but he is actually being **satirical**, or showing how absurd it really is.

Write with WORLD

UNIT 3 / LESSON 4
REVIEWING TEXTS
WRITING ABOUT CONTROVERSY

CAPSULE 1 3.4.1

THERE ARE TWO SIDES TO EVERY STORY, OR ARE THERE?

In Unit 1, you examined a controversial topic. You looked at two sides of an issue, but you didn't include your opinion. In this lesson, we'll examine what constitutes a controversy in more detail. And this time, you'll offer an informed opinion explaining what YOU think on the subject.

Typically, a controversy goes beyond a simple difference of opinion. A controversial topic may seem to have two "sides"—for instance people are either for or against elite sports. However, once you begin researching the controversy, you may find that within those broad categories of "for" and "against," there are lots of positions. Often, a controversy is a complex debate among several people or groups.

You might be surprised to learn that opinions about books have sometimes sparked major controversies. Consider Mark Twain's *The Adventures of Huckleberry Finn*. This book has been the subject of controversy since it was first published in the United States in 1885. A public library in Concord, Massachusetts banned the book that very year for its use of coarse language, such as the word "sweat" instead of the more refined option "perspiration."

This reason for banning, or prohibiting, people from reading the book may seem nonsensical to us, but since then the text has been banned numerous times. The reasons for banning Huck Finn have changed over the course of the last century, but even today there is continued debate about whether or not schools should require students to read this book. It actually holds distinction as the fourth most banned book in the United States!

The controversy surrounding *The Adventures of Huckleberry Finn* centers on Twain's stereotypical portrayal of African American slaves as, among other things, passive and ignorant. Furthermore, although some of the language he uses to refer to African Americans and Native Americans may have been commonplace in the late 1800s, it is now considered extremely inappropriate and degrading.

Even so, *Huck Finn* is considered one of the greatest American novels ever written and remains the most frequently taught work of literature after the works of Shakespeare. As we noted in 3.3.5, Mark Twain's works are particularly well-known for their use of satire to critique the failings of society. Huck Finn also has distinction as the first work of American literature to be written in the vernacular, or the language of the "common" man.

Given this information about the book, can you begin to imagine the various sides to the controversy and the people who represent those sides? Who might be offended by the teaching of *Huck Finn* in a middle school classroom? Why might they feel this way? Are there any groups who might believe differently? Why?

As you brainstorm, remember that there are always more than two sides to a controversial issue. Even if more than one group supports banning the book from the classroom, the reasons each group feels this way may be very different. For example, one group may believe middle schoolers are simply too young to understand Twain's purposes in writing and the book should not be taught until high school. Another group may believe the text is harmful and should not be taught at any level of education.

Use the following chart to help organize your thoughts.

People or Group	What is their (probable) opinion on *Huck Finn* being required reading for middle school students?	Why do you think they might hold this opinion?

It's time to start thinking about what controversy you want to write about in this lesson. But before you do, let's see what Jenny Pitcock has to say on the subject of controversy.

As well as being an author of *Write with WORLD*, Dr. Pitcock is a writer and editor for *God's World News*. In that role, she is occasionally called upon to cover controversial topics.

Here's how she approaches topics that elicit strong feelings among readers:

WORLD WISDOM

Animal testing. Gun control. The death penalty. These are all controversial topics, right? Yes. But as a writer for God's World News, *I've discovered they're not the topics that spark the most comments from our readers. You might be surprised to know that the topics we have to handle most delicately have to do with matters of faith and interpretation of the Bible.*

We get more letters and emails when we cover topics such as biblical creation or what constitutes a saint in the Bible than when we cover a traditionally controversial topic like abortion or euthanasia. Why is this true? Most God's World News *readers agree on issues the Bible clearly addresses, such as the sanctity of life. They also agree on essentials of the Christian faith, such as the omnipotence of God, the deity of Christ, his death and resurrection.*

But our readership is made up of Christians from a variety of backgrounds and denominations. We share faith; however, the way we understand Scripture may different slightly.

At God's World News, *we do our best to treat touchy subjects with care. That means when I approach a controversial biblical topic, I begin with much prayer. I want to show respect to all of our readers. Often that means we present a variety of positions without offering editorial comment on which one we personally adhere to. One goal we have for our readers is to understand all sides of an issue, not just the one they personally believe.*

CWJ

You are probably familiar with some of the big controversies that Dr. Pitcock mentioned. Controversies surrounding gun control, the death penalty, and animal testing have been debated for many years. These topics have been written about so extensively that it can be hard to narrow your research and write about them effectively. And, for the most part, none of them affect your life today.

◄ IN YOUR JOURNAL

Instead we suggest that you select a topic that is more relevant to you personally. Interests or passions you pursue outside the classroom— like music or sports —may be a great place to start your search. Here are a few ideas that may interest you as well:

► (At what age) should kids have their own cell phones?
► Are contemporary young adult novels (or TV shows or movies) too mature for tweens/teens?
► Are kids spending too much time on social networking sites (like Twitter and Facebook)?
► Do kids devote enough time to reading? Participating in outdoor activities?
► Is the current generation of kids too busy?
► Should families make quality time (eating meals together, attending church together, or "playing" together) more of a priority?
► Are schools (or parents or our "fast food culture") to blame for America's childhood obesity epidemic?

▶ Should schools teach cursive? Ban junk food? Give students more time for lunch and/or recess? Start later in the day or end earlier? Cut art and music classes? Limit homework?

▶ Should homeschooled students be allowed to participate in public school activities?

In your CWJ, write down any of these topics that interest you, as well as those you think of on your own. Try phrasing any new topics you come up with in question form.

Now read through your list and highlight the question you are most interested in. Spend some time reflecting on the controversy you choose by answering the following questions.

1.   Why are you interested in researching this controversy?
2.   What do you currently know about this controversy?
3.   Think of at least two groups of people that might hold different points of view on this issue. How do you think their opinions will differ?
4.   What are the "key words" of your controversy? (These will help you as you begin searching for sources.)
5.   What is your opinion on this controversy? Does anyone among your family or friends hold a different opinion than you do? If so, how are your views different?

CAPSULE 2   3.4.2

FINDING THE FACTS

By now you have selected a specific controversy to write about and reflected on what you currently know about the issue. Now it's time to find out more through research.

Here is the controversy I chose:

Should homeschooled students be allowed to participate in public school activities?

At this point, I could type the entire question into the search engine or pick a few key words. I selected "homeschooled students public school activities" and typed them into the tool bar.

My search brought up hits from the Home School Legal Defense Association, *The New York Times,* PBS, homeschool support organizations in various states, and private blogs.

At this point, I clicked on and began reading articles from the most reputable-looking sites. As I browsed through one article, I found that the most current thread of this controversy involves states considering passing laws that would allow homeschooled students to participate in public high school sports.

Here is a chance to narrow my topic and focus on an issue that is going on right at this moment. I replaced "activities" with "sports" and performed a new search. Among articles from several news sources and homeschool associations, I found this article from *God's World News*.

Homeschool Score

RICHMOND, Virginia—*Lawmakers in Virginia are taking on homeschoolers. The "Tebow Bill" cleared its first hurdle in the state's House Education Committee. House members voted 14-8 in favor of a bill to allow homeschooling students to participate in sports at their local public schools.*

The bill is named after Tim Tebow, quarterback for the Denver Broncos who was homeschooled in the state of Florida. He played football with his local high school team, took the University of Florida to a national championship, and won the Heisman Trophy.

The law would keep public schools from joining organizations like the Virginia High School League that prohibits homeschooled students from playing sports with public school teams.

Homeschooling parents pay the same taxes as parents of public school students. Those taxes help to fund public school sports. They believe their children have just as much right to participate in school sports as students who attend those schools.

Among those who testified in favor of the bill was Patrick Foss, a 17-year-old homeschooler ranked as the number 16 college soccer prospect in the nation by ESPN. He plans to sign a soccer scholarship at the University of Virginia. Patrick has played throughout the world as a national all-star, but was not allowed to play at his local high school.

Opponents of the law say that homeschoolers whose only link to the campus is the locker room and sports field would put a strain on the team's unity. They say that students who don't learn together will not bond as a team.

Scores of homeschooled children and their parents cheered as the committee voted in favor of sending the bill to the House floor. The bill should easily pass in the House. But it must also pass in the Senate before becoming law. If the Tebow Bill becomes law, Virginia would be one of 15 states that allows homeschoolers to play sports in local public schools.

After reading this article, I know several verifiable facts about the controversy.

▶ Lawmakers in Virginia are considering a controversial bill that would give homeschooled students the option to play on public high school sports teams.

► The bill is named for football star Tim Tebow who was homeschooled in Florida and allowed to play for his local high school team.

► If the bill is voted into law it will mean that fifteen states allow homeschoolers to join public school teams.

It would be easy to view this controversy as having only two sides: Either you are for the bill or you are against it. However, as in most true controversies, there are many different sides to this issue. Your job as researcher is to identify the various viewpoints and report on them.

In order to do so, we'll have to examine why this issue has caused controversy.

Let's go back to the article to identify the stakeholders who are mentioned and their various positions. Stakeholders are people or groups that have an interest or investment in the issue. They have something to gain or lose based on the outcome of the controversy.

People or Group	What is their opinion on homeschooled students playing public school sports?	Why do you think they might hold this opinion?
Virginia High School League	They work to keep home-schooled students from being a part of public school teams so are likely not in favor of the bill.	
homeschooling parents	They believe their children have a right to play on public school teams.	They pay taxes that help fund public school sports.
17-year old homeschooler	He testified in favor of passing the bill.	He is a nationally-ranked athlete who was not allowed to play at his local high school.
"opponents of the law"	They are opposed to passing the bill.	Because homeschooled players do not attend school with the other players, their presence makes it harder for the team to be unified.

Notice that one of the boxes is blank. This is because the article does not tell us why the Virginia High School League wants to keep homeschooled students out of public school sports. At this point, we can add "Virginia High School League" to our search terms to find more information about their position on the issue.

Also, the descriptor "opponents of the law" is a bit vague. Does this refer to public school parents, public school students, coaches, or administrators? We can do another search for "opponents of the Tebow Bill" to find out who specifically is opposed.

It looks like I need to do some more source-searching in order to get a fuller picture of the controversy.

Why don't you get started too?

CWJ

Type your research question from 3.4.1 or a few key words into your search engine to begin looking for sources. Make sure to look for sources that offer a variety of viewpoints. You may want to look for a mix of objective news articles that describe various people's opinions and editorial pieces that offer one specific opinion.

Print off or bookmark at least four sources.

On one page of your CWJ write "Basic Facts." Use this page to keep track of the facts of the controversy. Write down these questions, leaving space in between for your answers.
1.   What is the central issue people are arguing about?
2.   Who is involved?
3.   When and where is the controversy taking place?

As you read through each of your articles, highlight the names of people or groups you come across that are stakeholders in the controversy. Remember that stakeholders have something to gain or lose based on how the issue turns out.

Write the name of each person or group you find at the top of a blank page in your CWJ along with these two questions:
1.   What is their opinion on the controversy?
2.   Why do they hold this opinion?

Use the information you gather from your sources to answer these questions. Even if you think you know why a group may feel a certain way, don't just guess! Make sure you find the evidence stated in one of your sources.

◀ IN YOUR JOURNAL

ACT LIKE SWITZERLAND AND BE NEUTRAL

THE PROFESSOR'S OFFICE

 Perhaps you've heard the saying that you should never discuss politics or religion in polite company. Have you ever wondered why people avoid these topics?

It's because people tend to have very strong viewpoints on political and religious issues. Friendly discussions can quickly turn into heated arguments.

I've witnessed this more than once in the classroom. I even had one student become so angry during a discussion of a political candidate's views that he stormed out of the classroom and slammed the door behind him!

People often have such fixed opinions about controversial topics that they may find it hard to even listen to the opposition's point of view, let alone consider it. So, every semester I do an exercise to help students get more comfortable with the process of considering points of view they don't necessarily agree with.

When students enter the classroom, I introduce a controversy—like dorm curfews—that the majority of them are familiar with and almost assuredly have an opinion about. For simplicity's sake, I divide the class into two sides, asking students who are in favor of curfews to congregate on one side of the room and those who are opposed to the university's curfew rules to move to the other side. I ask the two groups to spend time discussing why they hold this belief among their group. Then I give the students a simple assignment:

Develop an argument for the opposite point of view.

Following a chorus of "Aw, mans!" accompanied by lots of groaning and complaining, students set to work. At the end of the class, each group selects a representative to share its argument. It never fails to surprise me how superbly the students articulate the opposing viewpoint. Even though they don't agree with it, when required to, they are able to explain it and show its merits.

My goal in doing this exercise is not to have students change what they believe, but rather to take the time to understand why other people believe differently.

Doing so also prepares students for writing tasks that require them to be neutral. Once they have argued in favor of a position they don't agree with, they find it much easier to report on that position without judging it, which is one of the characteristics of an effective writer.

The professor makes an important point here. Part of writing about controversy involves being able to set aside your opinion on an issue—for a period of time—so you can accurately communicate the various viewpoints that are represented within that controversy.

You may have noticed as you read the "Homeschool Score" article in 3.4.2 that the writer does not divulge her stance on the issue. Instead she concentrates on telling her readers (1) the facts of the case and (2) how different people and organizations feel about the bill under consideration.

Your goal when communicating other people's viewpoints should be to appear impartial. You'll know you have done a good job remaining neutral if your readers cannot tell which side of the controversy you support.

For example, here is my assessment of one group's position on the Virginia bill to allow homeschooled children to play on public school sports teams based on all of the research I conducted.

> *Perhaps not surprisingly, homeschooling parents are among the biggest champions of the Homeschool Sports Access Bill. For many, it is an issue of the government granting their children equal access. Homeschooling parents argue that their children should be allowed to play on public school teams because they pay the same taxes as the parents of public school students. Without the opportunity to play on these teams, homeschooled students don't have the same ability to earn athletic scholarships to college as their public school counterparts. Furthermore, homeschooled students in rural areas where there are no private sports teams aren't afforded the opportunity to play team sports at all if public schools deny them access.*
>
> *Some opponents of the bill fear that opening up public school sports to homeschoolers will flood the schools with thousands of homeschooled students hoping to take advantage of the bill. Public school parents worry that their children's spots will be filled by homeschooled children. However, homeschooling parents are quick to point out that in states like Florida where homeschoolers already have access to public school programs there were only one or two homeschooled students in each district who chose to participate. Parents of the homeschooled population also add that in smaller districts where schools sometimes have a hard time making up a team, the addition of their children will be an asset rather than a liability.*

Based on these two paragraphs, can you tell how I personally feel about the proposed bill?

In the first paragraph I offer a few opinions from homeschooling parents that I found in the articles I read. In the second paragraph, I show how these parents refute the arguments of public school parents, but I am careful not to take sides.

IN YOUR JOURNAL ▶

CWJ

In 3.4.2 you found your sources and organized the information according to each group and its stance on your issue. The next step is to perform a write-up. When you finish with the write-up you will have produced an objective, thorough explanation of the various sides of your controversy.

If possible, compose these paragraphs on the computer. After you are done, go ahead and print out two copies in preparation for your work in the next capsule.

1.   Use the page in your CWJ labeled "Basic Facts" to write a paragraph summarizing the controversy. Try to incorporate your research question as an introduction to the viewpoints that will follow.
2.   Select three people or groups from the lists you compiled in 3.4.2. For example, in addition to home-schooling parents, I could have selected legislators, public school parents, public school students, home-schooled students, or coaches.
3.   Write one to two paragraphs about each group. Be sure to explain (1) the group's opinion and (2) why the group holds this opinion. Make sure that you incorporate specific evidence from your sources such as quotes from the people involved or relevant statistics.

Remember—no matter what your stance is on the controversy, your job is to act like Switzerland and be neutral.

CAPSULE 4   3.4.4

A LITTLE DISTANCE GOES A LONG WAY

How hard was it to remain neutral as you wrote about the controversy?

If you have an investment in the controversy it may have been very difficult to keep your personal feelings and opinions from creeping into your writing. And that's perfectly normal.

This is one of the reasons we will encourage you to wait a period of time—we recommend at least twenty-four hours— before you look at your writing again. After taking a break from your writing, you can return to it with a fresh eye. With a little distance, you will be able to identify issues with your writing—such as instances when you accidentally reveal your opinion —that are harder to see when you are engaged in the process of writing.

You should have composed between four and seven paragraphs about your controversy and the various viewpoints of the people involved in the CWJ exercise for 3.4.3.

If it hasn't been close to twenty-four hours since you completed that writing task, eat a snack, read a book, or organize your closet and come back to this capsule when twenty-four hours have elapsed. If it has already been that long, you are ready to critique your work.

Grab a copy of your controversy write-up and a handful of colored pencils: purple, blue, orange, green, red, and pink.

As you read through each paragraph, use the designated pencil to "color code" your work.

▶ PURPLE—Underline your research question.
▶ BLUE—Circle any words or phrases that reveal your opinion on the issue. (Adverbs can be a major culprit here. For example, "Homeschooling parents rightly believe…." The word "rightly" suggests to readers that you agree with these parents.)
▶ ORANGE—Put a box around the name of the person or group that each paragraph discusses.
▶ GREEN—Underline sentences that identify WHAT the group's position is on the controversy. (You should have at least one green underlined sentence for each of the three groups you discuss.)
▶ RED—Underline sentences that explain WHY the group has this opinion. (You should have multiple red underlined sentences for each of the three groups you discuss.)
▶ PINK—Be on the lookout for the grammar issues we discussed in this unit. Circle any:
  – misplaced modifiers
  – wrong verb forms
  – wrong verb tenses

Your now-colorful composition should offer you a visual representation of what you have done well and what you still need to work on. We'll work on revising your write-up in your CWJ, but first you can take another break and let someone else do the work for you.

CWJ

Remember the second copy of your controversy write-up you printed out in the last capsule? It's time to find a trusted friend, sibling, parent, or teacher to share your work with.

Hand the second printout of your paper and colored pencils to your partner. Ask them to read and respond to your paper using the color-coding instructions provided in this lesson.

Once you have received your paper back, compare your color-coding with your partner's. What did you code the same? What did you code differently?

In your CWJ, write down a plan for revision. What parts of the paper did you and/or your partner identify as needing work?
▶ Did you incorporate a research question to introduce your controversy?

◀ IN YOUR JOURNAL

- ▶ Are there blue circles indicating places where you need to be neutral rather than opinionated?
- ▶ Did you clearly identify the person or group you discuss in each paragraph?
- ▶ Did you tell WHAT each group's position is on the controversy?
- ▶ Did you tell WHY each group feels the way it does?
- ▶ Are there any pink circles identifying grammar issues that need to be corrected?

Follow your plan for revision to improve your write-up.

CAPSULE 5 3.4.5

STATING YOUR POSITION RESPECTFULLY

Your patience is about to pay off. After remaining neutral for most of this lesson, it is your turn to tell what you think about this controversy.

Hopefully by now you have a pretty full picture of the various sides to the issue. Your research over the course of this lesson has transformed you from an interested party into someone who has the information and understanding necessary to offer a well-articulated opinion on the issue.

When you share your opinion, we want you to pay particular attention to how you do so. By now you know that controversies are controversial because people have extremely strong feelings about them. These feelings can lead people to make unkind comments about the opposition, "adding fuel to the fire" as the saying goes.

But as Christian writers we have a responsibility to offer our opinions in a respectful manner. In Philippians 1:27 the Apostle Paul reminds the Church that our words should reflect Christ to others: "Only let your conversation be as it becomes the gospel of Christ." Proverbs 15:1 offers us a clear direction for dealing with sensitive subjects: "A soft answer turns away wrath: but grievous words stir up anger" (AKJV).

Rather than stirring up anger, our goal should be to express our opinions in a way that makes others want to listen. Some ideas for achieving this goal include:

- ▶ Acknowledge when the other side makes a good point
- ▶ Show that you can understand why people may feel differently than you do
- ▶ Offer a possible compromise that could help everyone get some of what they want

For example, in writing my opinion about the bill to allow homeschoolers to play public school sports, I could acknowledge that public school parents who are opposed to the law offer compelling arguments for their position. Notice that I try to be respectful of this opinion even though I hold a different opinion on the issue.

> *As a public school parent, I can understand why other public school parents may have reservations about allowing homeschooled students to join our sports teams. All parents want their children to be treated fairly, especially at school. It does seem a bit unfair that homeschooled students would not have to meet the same attendance and grade requirements as public school students in order to be part of the team. But it also seems unfair for homeschooled students not to have the opportunity to play high school sports. This is where the cliché "Sometimes life isn't fair" becomes applicable. There may not be a way to make this situation completely fair for everyone involved, but it comes down to choosing the option that gives the most opportunity to the most kids. If we can agree that giving kids more opportunities is our goal, then the answer is to include homeschooled students in the public school athletic system.*

Did you also notice that I identify myself as a fellow public school parent in the first sentence of the paragraph? By doing so, I am declaring my positionality.

What is positionality? Put simply, it is the position you occupy in life. It is who you are.

One's positionality includes all the positions, or titles, one holds. Some of my positions include: female, mother, Christ-follower, writer, thirty-two year old, amateur baker, Sunday school teacher, and book club leader.

It is often important for writers to share their positionality with their readers. Why? Because it lets readers know where you are coming from.

For example, readers would most likely assume that I am a homeschooling parent when they see I am in favor of passing the law to include homeschooled children in the public school athletic system. However, when I tell readers that I am a public school parent who supports this idea, they may react differently to my argument. Perhaps other public school parents would be more willing to hear what I have to say because I have kids in public school too.

You see, when people write objective newspaper articles, they don't need to tell us who they are. However, when writers take a stance on the issue, they should explain their positionality to readers.

This doesn't mean telling every position you occupy. Being a book club leader or an amateur baker probably doesn't affect my opinion on the homeschooling sports bill. My position as a public school parent definitely does.

As you explain your opinion on your controversy, remember that in order to do so responsibly you should:

▶ Treat your readers with gentleness and respect
▶ Be honest about your positionality (where you are coming from) as a writer

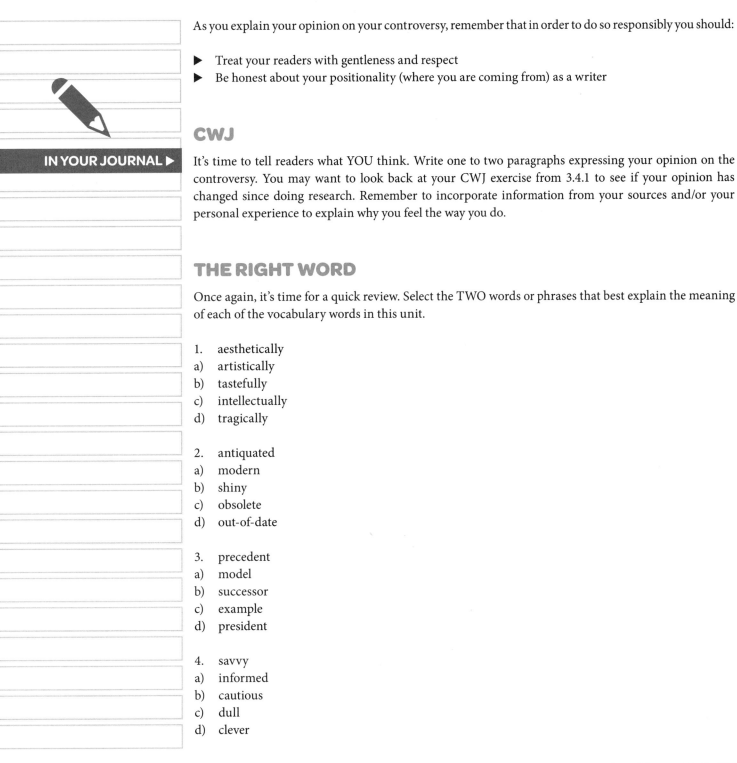

IN YOUR JOURNAL ▶

CWJ

It's time to tell readers what YOU think. Write one to two paragraphs expressing your opinion on the controversy. You may want to look back at your CWJ exercise from 3.4.1 to see if your opinion has changed since doing research. Remember to incorporate information from your sources and/or your personal experience to explain why you feel the way you do.

THE RIGHT WORD

Once again, it's time for a quick review. Select the TWO words or phrases that best explain the meaning of each of the vocabulary words in this unit.

1. aesthetically
a) artistically
b) tastefully
c) intellectually
d) tragically

2. antiquated
a) modern
b) shiny
c) obsolete
d) out-of-date

3. precedent
a) model
b) successor
c) example
d) president

4. savvy
a) informed
b) cautious
c) dull
d) clever

5. rapport
a) distrust
b) understanding
c) empathy
d) excitement

6. hedonistic
a) pleasure-seeking
b) stubborn
c) puritanical
d) self-indulgent

7. prolific
a) infertile
b) positive
c) productive
d) fruitful

8. affirmation
a) denial
b) confirmation
c) conflagration
d) assertion

9. zealous
a) fervent
b) apathetic
c) enthusiastic
d) poisonous

10. rebuke
a) admonish
b) reprimand
c) praise
d) squander

11. brevity
a) lengthiness
b) briefness
c) happiness
d) conciseness

12. proponents
a) advocates
b) suitors
c) detractors
d) supporters

13. synonymous
a) harsh
b) equivalent
c) dissimilar
d) interchangeable

14. satirical
a) mocking
b) sarcastic
c) approving
d) lazy

15. confound
a) clarify
b) confuse
c) construct
d) puzzle

Write with WORLD

CAPSULE 1

WHAT IS AN ESSAY?

In *Write with World II*, we've worked on developing opinions—and not just flippant, off-the-cuff ones. Rather, we've thought hard about topics and even done some research to make sure your opinions are informed opinions.

So far, most of the opinions you've developed and written about have been in response to someone else's ideas. That's a good place to start. Realizing that all ideas are part of a larger conversation among intelligent, thinking people helps you consider your audience as you write. Who might be reading your writing? Will your tone encourage them to keep reading? Or, like Professor Frop's, will it offend?

In this unit, we want you to learn to develop and write about your own opinions. That doesn't mean we expect you to come up with some unique, never-before-heard opinion on an obscure topic. We simply want you to think through a topic for yourself, form (or clarify) an opinion, and then provide logical reasons why you think your opinion is valid.

Most often, when we express our opinions in writing, we do so in the form of an essay. You may immediately think, "Yuck! I hate writing essays!" The word essay often inspires dread because it makes you think of boring, pointless assignments you've had to do in the past. An essay makes you think more of a to-do list than about sharing ideas or persuading someone to see a subject from your point of view. Here's what you may have learned: "An essay has to have an introduction with a thesis statement, three points, and a conclusion that restates the thesis and wraps up the essay."

That's one type of essay—the five-paragraph essay. We (both Dr. Pitcocks and Dr. Dietrich) have all written five-paragraph essays. Especially when writing an in-class essay, this pattern can help you make sure you're organized and you include enough points to satisfy your teacher that you know the material.

But an essay can be much more. Famous writer Aldous Huxley once said, "[T]he essay is a literary device for saying almost everything about almost anything." That's true. Essays have been written on almost any subject you can imagine.

Essays are usually short, but some are book-length. Historically, a few have been written as poems, though the vast majority are written in prose.

We hope you're getting the idea that a piece of writing called an essay can be many things. It doesn't have to be a mind-numbingly boring piece of writing you do for a grade. It should be writing that explores a single topic in a fresh, interesting way.

Rather than try to narrowly define an essay, we'll list some characteristics we think essays—whether they're five paragraphs or book-length, personal or more formal—must include to be effective:
▶ A well-supported opinion or position that makes readers think
▶ Some form of organization that is logical
▶ A distinct voice or style (unique way of saying things)

By the end of this unit, we want you to write an original essay—to share your opinion and get your readers to consider your views. We want you to write about some aspect of technology. We've purposely left the topic very broad so that you can choose something you really care about or are interested in. Today, in your CWJ, we want you to begin thinking about technology and brainstorming possible topics.

IN YOUR JOURNAL ▶

CWJ

Look up the word "technology." If you look at a few definitions, you'll see that this concept is hard to pin down! In general, we might say it's using scientific knowledge to benefit mankind in some way. It's also all the machines and devices that create those benefits. Air conditioning is a technology. So is a cell phone.

In the essay you'll be writing in 4.4, we want you to offer an opinion on a specific technology. The readings in this unit focus on computer technology, so that may be where you'll want to focus.

Today, in your journal:
1. Brainstorm a list of the technology you use on a daily basis—from cars to hairdryers.
2. Look at your list, noting especially the items having to do with computers, cell phones, and other communication technology. Circle any that are controversial.
3. Which ones cause personal controversy for you? Are there technologies that you would like to have but don't (your own computer or cell phone? A Facebook or Instagram account? Cable TV? A computer gaming system?), or those which cause conflict in your family or among friends? Write a sentence or two explaining one that causes conflict or controversy and why.

CAPSULE 2

TYPES OF ESSAYS

To recap, an essay is a piece of writing that explores a single topic. If you look at various textbooks and descriptions of essays, you might see a dozen or more different types of essays. But most of them can be grouped under three broad categories:

1)   Personal essay: This type of essay typically tells an autobiographical story. One purpose might be to entertain. But, like all the other types of essays, a good personal essay explores a single topic or theme. A personal essay will take a more informal tone, but typically the story or stories it tells explores a topic with a purpose, perhaps to share through the writer's experience what she has learned.

2)   Expository essay: This type of essay explains something. Lots of the essays students write in school are variations of this essay. Essays that compare and contrast two things or that explain how to make or do something are expository essays. This type of essay is based on facts.

3)   Persuasive essay: In a persuasive essay, the writer attempts to convince the reader of something. To do so, the writer must provide evidence to convince the reader (such as facts, personal experience, logical thinking, and expert witness or opinion). At the same time, the writer must take into account other people's opinions and viewpoints in a thoughtful, sensitive way.

Throughout the course of your life, you'll probably have occasion to write each of these types of essay. For school, you'll almost certainly write the last two types. In this unit, we want you to write a persuasive essay. We've been working up to it since the beginning of *Write with WORLD II*. Though there are good reasons to write each type of essay, our goal in this course has been to help you develop an informed opinion and your own unique voice—elements that are essential to an excellent persuasive essay.

We've told you that we want you to write a persuasive essay—but why should YOU want to? A few really brilliant people out there have the ability and focus to think through ideas in their minds and develop arguments without ever writing their ideas down. But for most of us, writing essays is a good way to examine, test, and refine our ideas. Our ability to think about a topic and delve into it more deeply is greatly enhanced by forcing ourselves to write it down and organize it logically.

And, as we've said before, as Christians, our conversations, both spoken and written, seek truth. We shouldn't focus on winning an argument for argument's sake, but rather on using argument to clarify our own and others' positions.

So far, that sounds about as fun as a spinach smoothie with extra vitamins—good for you, but a bit of a chore to swallow.

CWJ

That's why your work today in your CWJ is so important. We want you to see that there are things that you believe in and want in life. Sometimes, because you're a kid, you don't get taken seriously. We want you to realize that if you provide well-thought-out reasons, people will be more willing to consider your opinions. That doesn't mean you'll always get what you want—and sometimes, you shouldn't—but when you learn to make a persuasive argument, you have a much better chance of being heard.

Consider a time recently when you've tried to convince someone. Here are some possible situations you may have encountered:

1. You tried to convince your parents to let you go somewhere/participate in some activity
2. You wanted to download a particular song or watch a particular movie or show
3. You like a certain musical group or type of music and a friend or family member doesn't
4. You have a difference of opinion with someone on how much time should be spent using computer technology, watching TV, texting, etc.
5. You tried to convince your parents that you needed some new technology (computer tablet, phone or smart phone, a particular app, etc.)

Write up a short description of the discussion and the outcome.

CAPSULE 3   4.1.3

WHAT SHOULD I WRITE ABOUT?

In your CWJ last time, we had you consider a difference of opinion you've had with someone. Whatever the situation was, you felt strongly enough to express your opinion. That's how we want you to feel about the topic you choose for your essay. To be persuasive, you need to care. If you have no passion about your topic, you won't be able to convince anyone else to share your opinion.

That being said, we also want you to choose a topic that's current and relevant. If you are passionate about the beauty of Gregorian chants, that's wonderful. However, it's not a topic that lots of people currently talk about.

We've chosen the topic of technology because we think you'll have an opinion worth sharing about something in this broad category. For the rest of this lesson, you'll spend your time reading some articles from *WORLD Magazine*. We hope they'll spark some ideas that you might write an essay about.

WORLD WISDOM

To help you get started, *WORLD* writer Janie B. Cheaney shares how she comes up with ideas for her essays:

*"Where do you get your ideas?" Some writers roll their eyes when they hear that, but it's actually a **profound** question. What are ideas anyway? They are impressions, pictures, sounds and sayings that dance through our brains, and we catch them from each other, once they are put into words.*

Most of my ideas come to me through the Internet. I'm especially interested in education, arts and media, culture (how people think they should behave), and society (how they really behave). That covers a lot of territory! Sometimes I want to explore a topic, and an essay grows out of the exploration. Sometimes my thoughts are pretty well defined, and I see an article or an incident that backs me up. I usually start the week with no clue what to write about, but something always catches my attention.

Robert Louis Stevenson wrote, "The world is so full of a number of things, I am sure we should all be as happy as kings." The "things" in the world don't always make me happy, but there's more than enough to keep me busy. My job is to peel back a layer of it here and there, look a little more closely, connect this with that, and understand how it fits with God's truth (because everything does). And when somebody asks me that question, I often say, "I don't get ideas. Ideas get me."

CWJ

Mrs. Cheaney gets her ideas from reading on the Internet. Do you read the news? Newspapers, news websites, and television news are a good source for coming up with ideas to write about. They tell you what's going on in the world.

Today, we'll pick up a newspaper or go online (with a parent's permission) and read a story about technology. Many news sites have sections titled "Technology." If you don't find something interesting in that section, find the "search this site" box. Type in a topic that interests you like "social media" or "computer gaming" or "new technologies."

When you've finished, jot down your opinion about what the article says. For instance, if the article is about social media making people feel more depressed, you would say whether you thought that was true or not and at least one reason for your opinion. (Example: "I think reading people's Facebook pages could be depressing, because people tend only to put up their prettiest pictures. They share their good news more often than they share the bad things that happen. That might make other people believe their lives aren't as happy as their friends' lives, because the friends are only showing their "best" face on Facebook.")

◄ IN YOUR JOURNAL

FREEDOM, OPPORTUNITY, AND THE INTERNET

In 4.1.4 and 4.1.5, we've pulled together a couple of readings that we think might spark ideas for your essay. Even if this general topic doesn't appeal to you, don't skip the readings. I often find that a single sentence or even an interesting image gets me thinking about a related topic. Reading will get you thinking.

This excerpt is from the article, "From Pascal to Point & Click," by Chris Stamper. It first appeared in *WORLD Magazine* on July 31, 1999. Only part of the original article is reproduced here. And we've cut it a little and changed a few words to make it easier to understand.

Me and my machine

An **axiom** called Moore's Law says that computer speeds double and prices drop every 18 months. This means that each quarter's PC models are a leap above the last, but every machine purchased has a bad case of entropy. The typical automobile can last indefinitely as long as it is well maintained and driven safely, but computers become dinosaurs in just three or four years. Everything about computers is constantly changing.

Nothing ever stays the same. The biggest change in the computer world this decade, of course, is the overnight rise of the Internet. The invention of the World Wide Web by Tim Berners-Lee and the birth of Mosaic, the first graphical browser, led millions to spend hundreds and thousands of dollars just to get free stuff off the Net. The mass marketing of the Internet has changed the way people look at computers. The PC has gone from being a cranky servant in the den to being a replacement for the TV set. People can get practically anything they want over a dial-up connection. If it can't be downloaded, it can be charged to your credit card and shipped.

Friendship, love affairs, and even employment are being carried on over the Net through the ever-growing pile of chat software that lets people type at each other across the miles. People can run into a lot of mentally deranged weirdos this way, but they can also find that kindred spirit who shares their love of gourmet pizza, rubber stamping, or the philosophy of Gordon Clark. This endless silicon-based Turkish bazaar extends to the intellect, as everyone on the Net can publish his innermost thoughts. Anyone with a little learning can turn an idea into a website or a virtual community. Every possible opinion can be found out there since there are no gatekeepers and no laws (at least in the United States) controlling what can be said.

What it means

Computers are like Legos, Tinkertoys, and Play-Doh. Users can fiddle with them and push and pull until they have something really cool. The cultural mandate possibilities of all this technology have barely been explored. The lack of gatekeepers, for example, means there is nobody who can stop the Christian worldview from getting out to the world. If Gutenberg's revolution put Bibles in every house, just think what computerization can do.

A few people with the right ideas, good web design, and a little marketing savvy can have great success in this medium. The often discussed dangers of this medium can be overtaken with a resurgence of Christian culture. The Internet will only become more powerful over the next decade as it begins to absorb the usual functions of phone service and cable TV within itself.

Microsoft executives have long dreamed of hooking up every home appliance through one computer in the den. Already, America is being wired for broadband, better wiring for faster connections. Computers are speeding up people's day-to-day tasks, then slowing them down as they deal with all the new problems created by the system. This media revolution will both globalize and tribalize the people who use the technology. That makes the need for Christians to be salt and light to this new universe more urgent.

"Life, Liberty, and Faster Broadband?" by Alissa Wilkinson appeared in the April 19, 2011 issue of *WORLD*. Though short, this piece raises important questions about the Internet and human rights.

Do humans have a fundamental right to the Internet? In July, Finland was the first country to declare access to faster broadband Internet a legal right. Then in September, the UN's International Unit of Telecommunications supported a broader adoption of the idea, suggesting that governments ought to encourage access by making broadband service development easier and keeping taxes on broadband moderate. Now Brazil's senate is considering a bill that would declare that access to broadband is a social right under the country's constitution. Finland already had substantial infrastructure in place when its bill passed, but should Brazil's measure succeed, the country would need to make a serious investment in infrastructure and education.

Such a declaration may seem extreme. And yet, the idea is gaining traction. Around the world, the Internet's ability to promote free speech and foster social change is a hot topic: The recent uprisings in Libya, Egypt, and Tunisia, for instance, were fostered partially by citizens connecting through social networking tools. And China has come under fire for severely restricting its citizens' access to the Internet. As everything from education to communication becomes increasingly web-based around the world, access to the Internet will likely continue to be an important issue to policy makers.

CWJ

Today in your journal, we want you to do what you have in past units: write down any words, allusions or images you don't understand in the readings. Then look them up and put the definitions in your journal. Next, write a short (one or two paragraph) summary of each.

1. In "From Pascal to Point and Click," Mr. Stamper first gives some history on the Internet. Though it's rather dated, you can see that what he was talking about over a decade ago has happened.

In the next section titled "What it means," he tries to make sense of the culture. He says "the media revolution will both globalize and tribalize the people who use the technology." What does he mean? Why does this make it even more important for Christians to be salt and light in this new universe?

2. List one opinion that you either found in the article or thought of yourself while reading the article. Once you've written down the opinion, write down whether or not you agree with it and one reason why.

3. The central question of "Life, Liberty, and Faster Broadband?" is pretty clear. In fact, it's the first sentence of the article. Do humans have a fundamental right to the Internet? Write a sentence or two giving your opinion on this issue including at least one reason why.

CAPSULE 5   4.1.5

THE BIBLE AND TECHNOLOGY

"The Bible Unbound" by Mark Bergin appeared in the February 9, 2008 issue of *WORLD*. We've shortened it, simplified it, and added a heading to make it easier to read. Pay particular attention to all the questions Mr. Bergin raises. Almost any of these could be the starting point for an opinion paper of your own.

As new technology moves the text of Christian Scripture off the printed page and onto computer screens, mobile phones, and iPods, believers around the world are confronted with the reality that the word of God is not a leather-bound book—or even written words for that matter.

Many leaders in the Bible software industry celebrate that change in understanding. This change could increase the frequency with which people encounter the Bible. It places emphasis back on the message. It discourages the reverencing of particular **conduits** of Scripture at the expense of Scripture itself.

What's more, the power of the Internet to distribute God's word at affordable rates around the globe has energized many mission organizations. It has excited donors as they watch their dollars go much further in spreading of truth.

But with new technology comes new questions: Do Bible search engines, digital **lexicons**, and easy-click study notes promote laziness? Should Christians continue to learn and study Scripture in the original languages when simple software seems able to do the work for them?

Bob Pritchett, president of Logos Bible Software, contends that such powerful digital tools encourage scholarship rather than hinder it. "When pastors and seminary students use our software, they still spend 15 hours per week in Bible study but get three times as much done because it saves all the time of pulling the book off the shelves, looking in the index, and turning pages."

Historically, Christianity has driven many of the most important breakthroughs in communication technology. Both the book and the printing press resulted from efforts to preserve and spread the Bible's influence.

Tools or Distractions?

Sean Boisen, an information architect for Logos, envisions new Bible study tools building on the concept of zoomable user interfaces. He has developed a prototype for approaching text in the same manner that Google Earth navigates the globe. Laying out all of Scripture on a single canvas, Boisen believes, would allow users to zoom in or out for varying degrees of detail without sacrificing visual context as when flipping pages or reloading screens.

But, again, such innovations raise questions: Might software that promotes individual mastery of Scripture reduce the need for community study? And should Christians contribute to the culture's obsession with multimedia?

Mark Miller, the director of communications at City of Grace church in Mesa, Ariz., doesn't see it that way. He views digital technology and web applications as an unstoppable force. He thinks Christians must participate to remain relevant. Miller embraces social networking sites like MySpace and Facebook. He believes sites like these enhance community between believers and reach out to the unconvinced.

Taking a more critical approach, Zack Hubert, pastor of technology at Mars Hill Church in Seattle, cautions Christians against adopting the new definition of community made popular by online social networking sites.

"The whole 'friending' structure is a violation of core community principles. Nobody has 20,000 friends. If some people have their life on Facebook, as many college students do, and they've stopped there and aren't forming the real physical relationships where they can challenge each other, then that is a major detriment to the gospel and to culture," he says.

◀ IN YOUR JOURNAL

Hubert's vision for the web is built on connecting people locally—a neighborhood rallying to care for a single mom, a group of carpenters joining to learn how the Scriptures bear on their vocation.

Most ministers, including Miller, agree that the church should use technology differently than the secular world. Whether that difference is limited to content or includes structure is a point of some disagreement. Technology is morally neutral. But to the extent that it delivers the word of God, it is good.

In "Proceed with Caution," Janie B. Cheaney expresses a different perspective on this topic. In this article published in the April 25, 2011 issue of *WORLD*, she reflects on the possible downside of new ways of interacting with God's word. She fears technology will cause people to lose sight of the fact that the Bible is, first and foremost, God's communication to us.

You can tell you're getting old when your first reaction to new technology is suspicion:

"Look at all these kids 'friending' each other on Facebook. How can you be friends with somebody you never even met?"

"What's up with this email? Don't folks know how to write letters anymore?"

"What's this? A 'ball-point pen?' Look how it skips and jams-the old reliable ink pot never did that."

"Writing? What's wrong with memory?"

OK, so I'm getting old. But I'm also invested in books, both to read and to write, and "book apps" give me feelings decidedly mixed. On the book blog I write with Emily Whitten, I shared some of these feelings about an app version of *Peter Rabbit*, which gives a lovely interactive spin to the Beatrix Potter classic. And I do mean lovely—charming too. But, I'm afraid, deeply **inimical** to actual reading, at the very age when children ought to be developing a sense of how words shape ideas and images.

My feelings about Bible apps are mixed as well. What's not to like about the Glo Bible, with its HD video clips and maps, reading plans, animations, virtual tours, topical search engines, easy navigation, art images, and adjustable text? Nothing, really. I like it a lot. I can see how the Glo Bible, soon available for iPhones, can be taken anywhere and used as a study guide, a research text, and a witnessing tool. I can see how the digital generation has lost or is losing touch with traditional Bibles, which are bulky and require some preliminary work to understand. "More than a Bible"? I can see that too: According to the promo, it's a "media platform full of Christian resources, constantly updated." Is Glo, and similar applications, the "future of the Bible"? Probably so. And that I don't like.

Reading black letters on a white page has been in decline for decades, and every year there's more speculation that digital innovation has encouraged the decline. Thirty-somethings and up are accustomed to getting information from a printed page, but it's not certain that future generations will get the hang of it. To those who say that interactive reading is just another form of reading, I say, "No it's not." It's different, maybe even fundamentally different. It's input-based, in that the "reader" is shaping his own reading "experience." He's punching buttons to get the desired content, not taking time to have a conversation with the content as it is. He is acting on the media, rather than allowing the media to act on him.

For instance, the Glo tutorials show how to do a specific topical search for Bible passages. Say you want to look up the words of Jesus in John's Gospel, but you want only the words spoken by Jesus in Jerusalem during Passion Week. The Glo Bible lets you incorporate the Atlas lens, the Timeline lens, and the Topical lens to locate and highlight those passages. Cool!

But there's another method: read John 12-19. A red-letter edition may make it a little easier to find the actual words of Jesus, but they're easy enough to locate. Pay attention to context, crowd reaction, building themes. Let the Spirit talk to you, change you. It takes time to learn to do this, time that an iPad user with a busy index finger may not feel like taking.

Promotion for the Glo emphasizes using the Bible as a sourcebook for "answers for life's problems." But that's not all the Bible is, or not even chiefly what it is. It's God's communication to us. Too much cutting and pasting, clicking, sorting, and virtual touring can obscure that fact for a reader who's not already very familiar with the contents.

All technology involves trade-offs, some more consequential than others. The Glo Bible and other apps can be useful, even amazing supplements to Bible study, so more power to those who use them. I would just tell my young friends not to neglect the plain printed word. Don't expect an app to "bring the word of God to life." Only the Holy Spirit does that.

CWJ

1. Today, we want you to begin by looking up all words, allusions, and references you don't understand. Instead of summarizing each article, write a one-to-two sentence statement in which you say what you think the article or essay's main point is.

2. Underline all the questions in "The Bible Unbound." Offer a response or opinion on one of these questions. Write one sentence in which you answer the question and offer one reason supporting your answer.

3. Do you agree with Mrs. Cheaney's central point that too much technology can distract us from the fact that the Bible is God's communication to us? Have you personally had any experience using Bible apps? If so, did you find it helpful or distracting? Write a sentence telling whether you agree or disagree

◀ IN YOUR JOURNAL

with Mrs. Cheaney's opinion. Then give one reason for your opinion.

We hope that by the end of today, you have an opinion about some technology that you would like to write about. If not, keep thinking! We've included a list of ideas here that might help. What is your opinion on:

1. the positives or negatives of Facebook or Instagram or some other social media?
2. the age (or other milestone) a person should be allowed to have a cell phone (if you think people should have them at all!)?
3. the positives or negatives of computer gaming?
4. the positives or negatives of people's ability to access almost any information so easily using the Internet?
5. the impact technological advances (from microwaving to personal computing) have had on the modern world's ideas of work and work ethic?
6. the positives and negatives of personal computing devices like tablets, mp3 players, and handheld gaming systems? Kids and teens often multi-task, doing five or more things at a time. What impact does being constantly "plugged in" have on people?

We think most of you will be interested in writing about computers and the technology surrounding it. However, if you are a car aficionado, you might want to offer an opinion on whether you think smart cars are a good answer to the problems of pollution and fossil fuels, or if they just create a new set of problems of their own. That's fine. We really mean it when we say we want this topic to be your own. Being forced to write about something you don't care about generally produces papers that show your lack of interest.

Keep plugging away until you come up with a topic you want to spend some time thinking about. By the beginning of the next lesson, we want you to have an opinion you're ready to explore.

STYLE TIME: COMMAS TO AVOID CONFUSION

 Have you ever very lightly penciled a comma into a sentence? You're not quite sure if you need one, so you create one that looks like it might just be a stray pencil mark? Or perhaps you use commas like a pause button: Each time you pause for a breath when reading, you stick a comma in the text.

Commas can be confusing. Sometimes it's hard to make sense of when we should use these little marks. In this unit, we'll hit three major reasons we use commas. They don't cover everything, but they address the most common comma dilemmas.

Today, we'll look at the first rule:

1. Add commas to avoid confusion.

Use a comma to separate items in a series. Say for instance you have a list of kids that you're supposed to babysit: John Granger Mary Margaret and Bobby. How many are there? Depending on the number of commas, you could be babysitting anywhere from three to five kids:

John Granger, Mary Margaret, and Bobby
John, Granger, Mary Margaret, and Bobby
John, Granger, Mary, Margaret, and Bobby

Do you see why we need the commas? They help clarify. Without them, items (or in this case, people) run together.

Use a comma when directly addressing someone. If you don't set the name of the person being addressed off with a comma, your sentence takes on a whole new meaning.
Fred read your book.
When you add a comma, it's a completely different sentence:
Fred, read your book.
Here, the comma shows whether you're talking to Fred or about him.

Use a comma to prevent misunderstandings.
Children who can swim three laps.
This looks like a fragment. To make it a clear, complete sentence add a comma:
Children who can, swim three laps.

To help you remember how to use commas to avoid confusion, teach someone else. Choose one of the three uses of commas to avoid confusion and create an example sentence. Then explain it to a classmate, parent, brother or sister.

Here's an example of how you might get started:
You: Can you tell from this sentence how many kids I met today at my ballet class?
Today at my first ballet class I met Rose Mary Jane Cathy Anne and Sarah.
Student: Six.
You: No, actually, I met five. . . .

THE RIGHT WORD

Below are the five vocabulary words in context for this week. You should already have defined them in your journal as you found them in the reading.

1. Some writers roll their eyes when they hear that, but it's actually a **profound** question.
2. An **axiom** called Moore's Law says that computer speeds double and prices drop every 18 months.
3. It discourages the reverencing of particular **conduits** of Scripture at the expense of Scripture itself.
4. Do Bible search engines, digital **lexicons**, and easy-click study notes promote laziness?
5. But, I'm afraid, deeply **inimical** to actual reading, at the very age when children ought to be developing a sense of how words shape ideas and images.

Using your thesaurus, try to find the BEST word to replace the bold word in the sentence. If you aren't familiar with the meanings of all the synonyms for each word in the thesaurus, you may need to use your dictionary to look them up. That way you can choose the word that best fits the sentence.

UNIT 4/ LESSON 2

THE ESSAY

CREATING A THESIS STATEMENT

CAPSULE 1

4.2.1

TESTING YOUR OPINION STATEMENT

By the end of the last lesson, you should have formed an opinion on a topic relating to technology. If you've got an opinion you're interested in exploring, then you're ready to begin this lesson. As *WORLD Magazine* founder, writer, and editor Joel Belz recommends (3.2), it's useful to get into the habit of beginning with an opinion. And, as he cautions, we need to be willing to put that opinion through the wringer and see if it holds up. And if it doesn't we must be willing to shift our opinions to match the truth that we find.

By the end of this lesson, you will have developed a thesis statement. That sounds very formal, but it's really just your informed opinion and reasons that support your opinion—all stated clearly in a sentence or short paragraph. It's the core of your paper. It serves as a small "map" or blueprint—it tells readers where the paper will be taking them.

But to begin, you need to test your opinion. Does it hold up to **scrutiny**? All of us have probably held an opinion that, upon further consideration, we've had to revise. Perhaps an author you thought was a genius as a young kid no longer holds your attention. Or a television show you thought was brilliant when you were seven now seems boring. As we gain experience, our opinions sometimes change.

The same can be true as you consider a topic, discuss it with others, and read about it. As you become more informed, your opinion often shifts at least slightly. Today, we want you to begin testing your opinion.

WORLD WISDOM

Before Dr. Jenny Pitcock was a writer and editor for *God's World News*, she was a student. She loved her literature classes because she loved to read. She chose her topics for writing based on ideas she knew she could prove. For her, writing wasn't about exploring ideas; it was about making sure she had the answers.

"I don't care if your paper is a failure," said Dr. Swingle. "What I care about is that you really explore a question." I had gone to college for four years and a Master's program for two more. I was in my third year of my Ph.D. program, and I had never heard anything like this. I always came up with my ideas for term papers by collecting evidence FIRST.

For me, coming up with a paper topic and thesis statement was an exercise, kind of like fill in the blank: "Hamlet's fatal flaw is an inability to take action, which is evident in _____, _____, and _____." I was good at coming up with thesis statements. Sometimes I had interesting, original ideas. My professors liked my writing. I was very thorough. I wrote about ideas I could easily defend.

Dr. Swingle's way of doing things threw me off balance. We turned in a research question early in the course. He asked questions in return until he thought we had something interesting—an original idea he hadn't seen before, something that proved we were really thinking.

In Dr. Swingle's class, I learned to write to explore an idea rather than to show what I knew. I learned not to be afraid of questions that don't have pat, easy answers. I learned to take risks. Without Dr. Swingle's class, I doubt I'd be a writer today. I'd never have moved past those safe class essays that didn't really require me to think.

CWJ

IN YOUR JOURNAL ▶

Your first task is to write down your opinion in a simple sentence in your CWJ. For instance, if you are writing on teens and multitasking, you might write, "I think my generation's ability to multitask is making us more productive."

Next, you'll need to find three willing participants. They should be close to your age or older and include at least one adult.

Have a conversation in person, by phone, or by email or text with each of your three participants. Ask them their opinion about your opinion statement. Do they agree or disagree? In as much detail as possible, write down their opinion and their reasons for their opinions in your CWJ.

Here's an example to get you started. "I sent my mom an email asking her what she thought of my opinion statement. Here's what she said. 'I definitely DON'T agree that your opinion statement is true. When you go in your room to do homework and you are texting friends at the same time, it takes you longer to finish. Especially with math, you get more answers wrong. That's exactly why I hold onto your phone until your homework is finished each day.'"

CAPSULE 2

4.2.2

WHAT ARE YOUR REASONS?

So how did your test go? Did your reviewers agree with your opinion? Or did they oppose it? Did the responses make you rethink your position?

If you've changed your opinion a little—or a lot—as a result of your test, that's a good thing. You engaged in conversation, and you listened to other opinions. You thought about what someone else said, and you realized your opinion needed revision.

If your opinion has changed, go ahead and revise it in your CWJ. Or if you've decided that opinion won't work at all, you might need to come up with something completely different.

Once you've solidified your opinion statement, the next step is identifying reasons for your opinion. For instance, if you think you are more productive when multitasking, why do you think so? Be honest. Do you really think it's true, or is it just more fun to text, listen to music, and watch TV while you are doing homework?

If you can't come up with any good reasons, that may mean your opinion statement is JUST an opinion and won't make it to the next level. An opinion is sometimes simply how you feel or what you like or what you think. A claim in a persuasive paper like you are writing is more than that. It's a well-considered opinion that can be supported and defended by solid reasoning, research, experience, or evidence.

"By the time kids are 13, they're old enough to have cell phones," is an opinion statement. But can it be turned into a **viable** claim? Tying a privilege to a particular age can make a claim difficult to prove. Think of the 13-year-olds you know. Chances are, you can think of some who are mature beyond their years. You may know others who act more like ten-year-olds. Consider your opinion carefully. Often, with a little rethinking and rewording it can be made into a workable claim. But be careful—if your opinion is tied to something that's going to be hard to defend (age, things that are personal to you such as your taste or style, etc.) you may need to make some changes before adding your reasons.

CWJ

Today, rewrite—and if necessary—revise your opinion statement into a claim. Once you've done that, answer the question "why." Give at least two reasons for your opinion.

◄ IN YOUR JOURNAL

For instance, with our sample claim, ""I think my generation's ability to multitask is making us more productive," we might give these reasons:

Why?

#1 My own experience has been that listening to music while I work actually helps me tune out other distractions and focus on my work.

#2 Many of the texts and emails I send and receive while doing homework are from friends doing the same subject. We ask each other questions and help each other. This allows us to finish faster and understand the material better.

CAPSULE 3 4.2.3

JOINING THE CONVERSATION

If you haven't done so already, it's time to do a little research. What do other people have to say about your topic? Your own experience can offer insight into an issue, but it's not enough. For instance, maybe you are the exception rather than the rule. Most kids who play video games for hours each day don't end up becoming video game designers. If you have designed a game and sold it to a company, you are the exception.

Or maybe you are just wrong. Let's look at our multitasking claim. Once we began to research, we found lots of evidence that says that people can't truly multitask. They can do something that they've done over and over again, like chop an onion while talking or walk while talking. However, if anything new is added—like changing directions or chopping something less familiar, like an avocado—people have to stop and think. Once thinking is involved, people are done multitasking. We cannot think of two things at once. We can toggle (switch back and forth) between two tasks but we can't truly do both at the exact same time.

Today's young people are extremely good at switching among activities, but some researchers think this is potentially damaging in the long run. It may shorten attention spans, among other problems.

Because such intense multitasking is a relatively new phenomenon, there's not a lot of proof about its effects. And a few people think multitasking is a good skill to develop, because it prepares kids to multitask at the jobs they will hold in the future. However, early research seems to point more toward problems multitasking causes than benefits it offers.

Once you've joined the conversation and seen what other people have to say about your topic, it's time to consider your thesis again.

CWJ

In *Write with WORLD II*, we've given you some tips on how to research a topic. You might want to review these sections if you aren't sure where to begin. It might be a good idea to tab the pages with post-it flags so that you can easily flip to them:

Unit 1.3.4

Unit 1.4.2

Unit 3.2.3

Unit 3.4.2

Unit 4.1.3

If you find some articles that contain convincing evidence, such as research and studies or expert opinion, you may want to print them out or bookmark them on your computer. You'll need them for the next capsule (even if you still don't agree with them).

After you've looked at the research, write a short paragraph telling whether or not your opinions and reasons are changing, and if so, how. Share a little of your thought process. For instance, on the multitasking topic, our writer might say, "I still feel like I work better when I'm multitasking, but the evidence mostly says that's not true. I think I need to read some more on this topic. Maybe I'll try an experiment myself where I don't multitask and compare the experiences."

◀ IN YOUR JOURNAL

CAPSULE 4   4.2.4

ORGANIZING YOUR RESEARCH

In the last capsule, you gathered some research. In this capsule, we'll work on getting it organized so that you can carefully consider it. Is there an opinion that a **preponderance** of the evidence seems to support?

In the sections we pointed you to in your CWJ (4.2.3), we've offered you some tools for organizing what you read. You might like to make a chart like this one:

Author	What is the author's opinion or which position does the article support?	What reasons or evidence do they offer for their opinions?

Another option is to make a Pros/Cons list. (For example, what do the articles say is good about multitasking? What do they say is bad?) In our opinion, the best way to make sure you keep your facts straight is to 1) quote exactly from the article when possible and 2) write down the author's name (and page number if there is one). Regardless of whether you do a chart, list, or some other method that works for you (Notecards? A giant whiteboard?), make sure you very carefully keep track of where your information came from.

Next, consider any personal experience you have with the technology itself. Is there an experience you could include in the paper? For instance, if your grades have gotten better since you started multitasking, you might include that personal example.

What about logical reasoning? For instance, adults at their jobs are often required to multitask. Doesn't it seem that students will be better prepared for the work force if they can effectively do more than one thing at once?

Today in your journal, we want you to gather all the reasons you can find that support your opinion—research, experience, and logical thinking.

CWJ

IN YOUR JOURNAL ▶

Remember, your goal in writing an opinion paper is to seek the truth. That means that you may need to begin adjusting your thinking at this point. If there is just one small article that supports your opinion and pages of evidence to the contrary, you're not seeking truth if you cling to your opinion despite your findings.

Today, in your CWJ, we want you to think on paper. It may surprise you, but a great deal of the thinking and preparation for writing must be considered before you develop your thesis statement. You have to have an idea of where you're going. It still can change—you may even do a U-turn and switch directions—but by the point at which you create your thesis statement, you should have thought about your topic a great deal already.

In your journal today, we want you to organize your research. In the first section, organize the articles you read. If you've got it in great detail somewhere else that works better for you, like a white board, that's fine. If so, summarize your findings in your journal. Otherwise, create a chart or list here.

In the second section, brainstorm any personal experiences or experiences of those you know that you could include. This section could also include personal research—interviews with experts or others who might offer support for your position. You could even consider experimenting with the technology yourself in some way. For instance, using our multitasking example, you could set up an experiment where you tried working with and without multitasking and compared the results.

In the third section, think through possible logical reasons your position is true. Consider at least one line of thinking that seems to prove your point. (Example: Whenever new technologies are introduced, people are suspicious of them. But God made us very **resilient** and adaptable. So far, technology and its impact haven't had the dire effects that are constantly being predicted.)

CAPSULE 5
4.2.5

DEVELOPING YOUR THESIS STATEMENT

In the last few capsules, you've done lots of thinking and researching about your topic.

Today, we want you to work all of your thoughts into a sentence or short paragraph. Most essays have a thesis statement of some type. This serves as the "map" of your argument. It helps your reader figure out and then follow your reasoning.

Depending on the type of paper you're writing, a thesis statement may take different forms. In all, it reveals the central message of your essay. However, if you are writing an expository essay on how to make a peanut butter sandwich, it's going to be a different type of thesis statement than you would come up with for a persuasive essay.

Because you'll be writing a persuasive essay, your thesis statement will be a claim (informed opinion) and the reasons supporting your claim. In a persuasive paper, your claim needs to be controversial. For instance, "video gaming is very popular" is both vague and a fact—not something that someone could take another position on. On the other hand, "Video gaming can teach critical thinking," is an arguable claim. Can you see the difference? One is a fact; the other is a position that people hold opposing views on.

Once you've stated your claim, in a few sentences, lay out the rest of your reasons. "Some video games promote critical thinking. Gaming often involves having to make quick judgments based on what you see on the screen. Many require logic and puzzle-solving skills. The government has even created video games to help U.S. spies improve their critical thinking skills."

When you've done this, you've got the basis for your persuasive essay. This thesis statement provides you and your reader a map of where the paper is going. You can develop each of these points, using logic and personal experience as well as the research you have **garnered** in this lesson.

IN YOUR JOURNAL ▶

CWJ

Today, we want you to write your thesis statement, which will be made up of a claim (informed opinion) and the reasons for your opinion. Use the example in today's capsule as a model.

Once you get it into a short paragraph, see if you can reduce it to a single sentence. You may end up using the longer form, but often teachers require a single thesis sentence, so it's good practice.

Here's what the example thesis statement might look like if reduced to one sentence: "Some video games promote critical thinking because they force players to make quick judgments and require logic and puzzle-solving skills; the U.S. government has even created video games to help spies learn the critical thinking skills they will need in their jobs."

We think this thesis statement works better as at least two sentences, and yours might too. But working it down to one sentence encourages you to make sure your points are worded in a parallel way and all make sense together.

STYLE TIME: COMMAS – THE FANBOYS RULE

 You have probably seen the FANBOYS acronym before. It's made up of the first letter of all of the coordinating conjunctions:

For
And
Nor
But
Or
Yet
So

These conjunctions can be used to join two independent clauses. A comma should be placed BEFORE the coordinating conjunction. Here's an example:

I think my thesis statement is spectacular, and I can't wait to write my persuasive essay.

The exception is very short sentences. In these, the comma is optional:
I ate and then I left.

However, if you're not sure, err on the side of caution. You're never wrong to use a comma before a coordinating conjunction that joins two independent clauses.

Caution: Make sure you have a compound sentence and not simply a compound verb. We often see sentences like this one:

I ate dinner, and then played basketball.

If there is no subject after the conjunction, you don't need a comma.

Correct:

I ate dinner and then played basketball.

OR

I ate dinner, and then I played basketball.

See if you can find the spot in this lesson where we've left out a comma before a coordinating conjunction (Hint: Look at 4.2.3).

THE RIGHT WORD

 Below are the five vocabulary words in context for this week. You should already have defined them in your journal as you found them in the reading.

1. But to begin, you need to test your opinion. Does it hold up to **scrutiny**?
2. But can it be turned into a **viable** claim?
3. Is there an opinion that a **preponderance** of the evidence seems to support?
4. But God made us very **resilient** and adaptable.
5. The writer could develop each of these points, using logic and personal experience as well as the research he has **garnered** in this lesson.

Using your thesaurus, try to find the BEST word to replace the bold word in the sentence. If you aren't familiar with the meanings of all the synonyms for each word in the thesaurus, you may need to use your dictionary to look them up. That way you can choose the word that best fits the sentence.

UNIT 4/ LESSON 3

THE ESSAY

CONSIDERING AUDIENCE, TESTING ARGUMENTS

WHAT WRITERS WILL NEED FOR THIS LESSON:
▶ Your writer's journal
▶ Dictionary
▶ Thesaurus
▶ Post-it flags

CAPSULE 1

4.3.1

WHY ARE YOU WRITING?

"Please pick me up. Practice is over!" you might text to your mom. "Thanks for all the birthday wishes—I had a great day!" you might post on a social networking site. Most of us frequently write to many different audiences with different purposes. Often the **missives** we send are short and to the point, with a clear message. Most often, we write to communicate, to share information. All of the writing that we do has one thing in common—we write to someone or with someone in mind.

Even if you keep a journal, you have an audience: Yourself. Whether you plan to keep it and look back on your life someday or you read back over it now, you're writing with a purpose and an audience in mind.

In fact, whether it's a grocery list, a Post-it note on the cookies you made for a bake sale saying "Do not eat!" or an online update, we challenge you to find writing that isn't geared toward an audience.

In real-life writing situations, we instinctively write to someone. In your persuasive essay, you should be writing with someone in mind. Otherwise, it's just a collection of information with no purpose. It's hard to get excited about merely collecting information if no one is going to read it.

A persuasive essay is a type of argument. We don't mean the kind of knock-down, drag-out fight that involves anger and name-calling. We mean logical reasoning with the intent to discover the truth on a subject.

If you are writing with no specific audience in mind, you can't craft your best argument. Think about it: Reasons that would be persuasive to your friends would be different than those that would persuade your parents.

So we'll begin this lesson by thinking about to whom you should direct your essay.

CWJ

Answer these questions in your CWJ:

1. What person or group can you think of who would probably agree with your thesis statement? In other words, who would be on the same side of the argument as you are?

2. What person or group would probably disagree? Why do you think (or know) they would disagree?

3. Once you've determined a person or group you think would oppose you, look at your thesis statement. Do you think you've chosen reasons that would convince this person/people? Why or why not?

CAPSULE 2   4.3.2

RHETORICAL SENSITIVITY

Rhetoric is the art of speaking or writing effectively. If you look up this word, you'll see that this word has even more to it—especially as it relates to the history of speech and writing. The main point we want you to consider in this capsule is that a huge part of speaking and writing effectively is not offending your audience.

In the last capsule, you should have chosen an audience who doesn't believe as you do about your topic. Even so, you want to make sure you're respectful in your tone. If anyone has ever laughed at some opinion or idea of yours, you know how hurtful it can be. Taking a mocking or condescending tone won't win over your readers. If anything, it will make them cling more tightly to their own ideas.

At the same time, we want you to confidently stand up for what you believe in, even if it's controversial. As *WORLD* correspondent Amy Henry reminds us, we need to be sensitive and careful. But that doesn't mean we avoid difficult topics. She offers advice on how to handle hard subjects with grace.

WORLD WISDOM

There are times when I know that the essay or blog post I am writing will be controversial. In these instances, I usually start out with a note to let my audience know that I know we are on shaky ground. Establishing that from the beginning helps readers know I am aware that the issue is sticky. This can prevent a flood of responses from people who just assume I am clueless.

Sometimes, something I've written is simply misunderstood. It's best not to take it personally and get huffy about it, but to respond (as we at WORLD are encouraged to do in our writer's guidelines) with kind and gentle explanation. This diffuses conflict in most situations, while respectfully addressing the reader's concern.

At still other times, I run into Internet 'trolls' or readers who seem bent on picking a fight, who take my words out of context, or skew them to mean something I never intended. In these cases, I refuse to engage. These readers are usually not as interested in clarifying things as being a rabble-rouser. In my experience, these sorts of 'debates' simply raise your blood pressure and keep you so busy defending yourself that you have no time for writing.

So, to sum up: Begin with a note to let your reader know you are aware the topic is controversial. Kindly clarify if you are truly misunderstood. Don't lose any sleep over chronically nit-picky readers. Good writing will sometimes offend people. You simply cannot please everyone, especially when you are taking a stand on an issue. Consider carefully what you are trying to say, and make certain you think your piece accurately represents what you believe.

THE PROFESSOR'S OFFICE

When I teach students how to write arguments, one of the most important lessons they learn is rhetorical sensitivity. To be an effective writer of arguments, you need to understand your audience.

Anyone can say what they believe—absolutely anyone. A smaller number of people are able to state belief and explain it clearly. But only an elite group of writers can share beliefs and ideas in a way that is savvy. By savvy, I mean well informed and having a sense of their audience's thoughts. I want you to be this savvy writer; I want you to practice rhetorical sensitivity when writing arguments.

When you write arguments for a specific audience, you need to know their interests and beliefs. Where do they stand on a controversy and why? What is important to them? What do they know and why might they not agree with you based on their knowledge? How do they not understand you? Once you understand your audience, you can adapt your writing to address their needs, develop a strategy that will motivate them to read your writing carefully, and ultimately help them hear your message.

Ten years ago I worked with a student named Amy who was a Christian, and Amy wanted to write about a controversial topic that many Christians care about—a topic on which the Bible takes a firm stance. Amy's essay was well organized and had a strong statement of belief. Her reasons were supported almost entirely with Bible verses—at least 20 of them.

Now, Amy's essay made complete sense to me: as a Christian I understood her thinking and valued the Bible verses she chose. I personally thought her essay was clear and persuasive.

But I—a Christian professor—wasn't Amy's audience. I believe in the Bible and think in a similar way. Her audience did not.

Amy wanted to persuade people who disagreed with her. The people she desired to reach were not Christians—some of the people in her audience were likely anti-Christian and violently opposed to her. They did not believe the Bible as Truth. More than likely, her audience would have been highly offended by her large use of Bible verses—they would have seen it as extreme and defined Amy's paper as having poor logic. My guess is that they would never finish reading her paper.

To make the paper better, Amy needed to understand her audience better. Her audience wanted to hear scientific facts and medical studies. They would be more open to hearing stories from people with relevant experiences and interviews with doctors. Amy needed to rewrite her essay to incorporate different types of evidence. She needed to rewrite the paper to become rhetorically sensitive to her audience's needs.

Amy also needed to think about her use of Bible verses. In this instance, one or two strategically placed verses could have a greater impact on her audience than the 20 Bible verses she used in the essay I read.

Amy rewrote the paper, and the process was a difficult one. She revised the paper to do more than state her belief. She wrote a paper that was rhetorically sensitive: a work designed to share her ideas in a way her audience might read. And it worked!

Three weeks after finishing her paper, the student shared her revised and rhetorically sensitive paper with her college roommate, Emma. Emma was not a Christian and represented Amy's audience perfectly. Emma read the entire paper. Though Emma disagreed with Amy's belief, she had questions about Amy's evidence and wanted to discuss the two Bible verses. Over the course of six weeks, Amy and Emma had a lot of discussions concerning the paper, their ideas on the topic, and the Bible verses.

Because Amy revised the paper to be more rhetorically sensitive and used evidence that her audience would be open to considering, she was able to clarify her ideas to Emma and have a mature conversation. Good arguments should create meaningful and mature conversations.

CWJ

IN YOUR JOURNAL ▶

The audience you chose in 4.3.1 should be someone you really know. You should be able to, in your mind, have a conversation with this person. Consider one of the reasons in your thesis statement. If you were to have a conversation with them about it, what would they say? (If they were one of the participants in your opinion statement test, look at what they had to say.)

Today in your journal, write up an imaginary talk with that person. You may be thinking, "But I could just ask this person. Why have an imaginary conversation?" You don't always have the luxury of speaking with the person whom you're trying to convince. I think most professional writers carry on a running dialogue with their audience. We're constantly trying to anticipate how our audience will respond. Learning to think like your audience is necessary to good writing.

As you converse:
1. Ask him what he thinks about your topic.
2. Write how you think he would respond.
3. In a respectful way, offer your counter opinion.

Here's an example:
If we chose a friend to be our audience for a persuasive essay on the downside of multitasking, here's what our imaginary conversation might look like.

Student: So do you think you're good at doing more than one thing at once—like texting and listening to music while doing your homework?

Friend: Yeah, I'm usually doing at least three things at once—and I always get everything done.

Student: I know you can do it—and that you get good grades. Have you ever tried to do your work in peace and quiet? Unplugged everything?

Friend: No. I'd get so bored. I need lots of activity. It helps keep me alert.

Student: That's how I feel too. But I've been looking at some interesting research on the subject recently—it says that the long-term effects might be bad for our brains. If you knew it were doing damage to you, would you consider working without so many distractions?

Friend: I think I'm fine—but I guess if someone proved it to me, I mean, I don't want brain damage or anything.

CAPSULE 3

4.3.3

WHERE DO WE AGREE?

In the example in the last CWJ, our writer did some things that you will need to do in a successful persuasive essay.

1) She validated what her friend had to say—"I know that you can do it." This shows that she's listening AND that she's willing to acknowledge her friend's position has some merit. It's absolutely true that

many very good students get everything done—with stellar grades—while multitasking.

2)   She acknowledges that she feels the same way. Remember in Lesson 3.4.5 when our writer reveals she is a public school parent in favor of allowing homeschoolers to play public school sports? She's using that information to build trust and credibility with readers who, as public school parents, may not agree with her. Any time you can establish common ground with your readers, it helps set the stage for persuasion.

3)   Finally she finds an assumption that people on both sides of the argument can agree on: That doing harm to your developing brain is bad. Shared assumptions are key to developing a persuasive argument.

In Unit 3, we did a great deal of thinking about being sensitive to audience. In 3.4.5, we shared some ways to show respect. You can acknowledge when your opposing side has a good point.

You can show that you understand why people may feel differently than you do. These are both ways to demonstrate that you have considered your audience's viewpoint. In writing, this is how you demonstrate "listening."

These steps are a good start toward being persuasive. You will never convince your readers by treating them disrespectfully and ignoring their opinions. But to be truly persuasive, you need to go one step further: You need to discover the arguments that will sway your audience.

So how do you find these? If you know your audience well—like you do your parents—you've figured out what persuasive tactics are most convincing. If you're asking them for permission to go out with friends, how would you approach them? Would you clean your room first? Start with a little speech reminding them about how responsible you're getting to be? Promise to stay with the group and keep your cell phone turned on so that they can reach you at all times?

When making an argument for your readers, you need to consider what arguments will be most persuasive to that particular group. Take for instance our multitasking example. If your audience is other preteens and teens, they probably aren't going to be motivated by the impact multitasking is going to have on them 20 years from now. You need to find arguments that make a difference to them now.

One way to do that is to find shared assumptions—things everyone can agree on. If you build your arguments (or at least some of them) on these shared assumptions, you have a better likelihood of convincing your reader.

Today, in your CWJ, we want you to find some assumptions that you think both you and your audience can agree on.

CWJ

In your CWJ today, write your thesis statement. As you look at it, can you think of anything that a person must assume in order to believe your argument?

Let's take a look at this sample thesis statement so we can show you what we mean:

> I believe that constant multitasking is more harmful than beneficial. Some studies show that multitasking could be preventing young brains from developing important connections. It also slows teens down as they work and decreases their ability to focus.

Here are some assumptions the writer is making:

▶ We want our brains to develop the proper connections
▶ Efficiency (not working slower) is good.
▶ Being focused is important.

We think these are assumptions that both the reader and the writer could share. We can't imagine that anyone would want to do harm to their brain. We also think most people would want to finish quicker (though some students might think it's better to enjoy themselves and take a little more time.) Most teens would agree that it's important to be able to focus, too.

Consider your thesis statement.
List at least two assumptions you are making. Do you think your audience would agree with your assumptions? If not, what other reasons might you consider including in your thesis instead?

◀ IN YOUR JOURNAL

CAPSULE 4   4.3.4

REBUTTAL: REFUTING AN OPPOSING VIEW

In your CWJ for 4.3.2, we had you imagine a conversation with your audience. In it, you should have envisioned what they might say in response to your position. Why do they not agree with you? What argument will they make in response?

In this capsule, we want you to consider an important feature in persuasion that you may not have thought about before. In order to persuade someone to your position, you need to show them how their current position is flawed.

In an argument, the section where you **refute** another argument is called rebuttal. You rebut an opponent's position by offering a counterargument or proof that their argument isn't true or that its logic is flawed.

So how might this work? In the persuasive essay example we've been working with, the writer is trying to persuade friends that multitasking is more harmful than beneficial. In 4.3.2, she identified the main argument she thinks her friend would make in favor of multitasking—it keeps them alert and prevents them from being bored.

If this writer can refute this argument in some way, she has a better chance of persuading her friends to her position.

This is a difficult one, because it's based on her audience's experience. They know it's more boring to work without all the distractions. So in this case, she's probably going to have to show that while they may feel more alert, they are actually less so, because their attention is going in so many different directions.

What are some ways she might be able to convince her audience? She should probably go to her articles first. Are there any studies that show that students are less alert when multitasking? If she can find proof, that helps. Even so, she is going to deal with the issue of exception. We often think we're the exception to the rule. Her audience might think, "Most people may not be able to handle multitasking, but I can." Here, she might add in a personal experiment where she tells about how she decreased her homework time and increased correctness and focus by eliminating multitasking. She might challenge her audience to try the same experiment.

Do you see what we're getting at here? You can write a whole essay that has strong points, but if you don't ever address the reasons your audience believes their thoughts are right—in this case, their arguments in favor of multitasking—you will almost certainly fail to persuade them.

CWJ

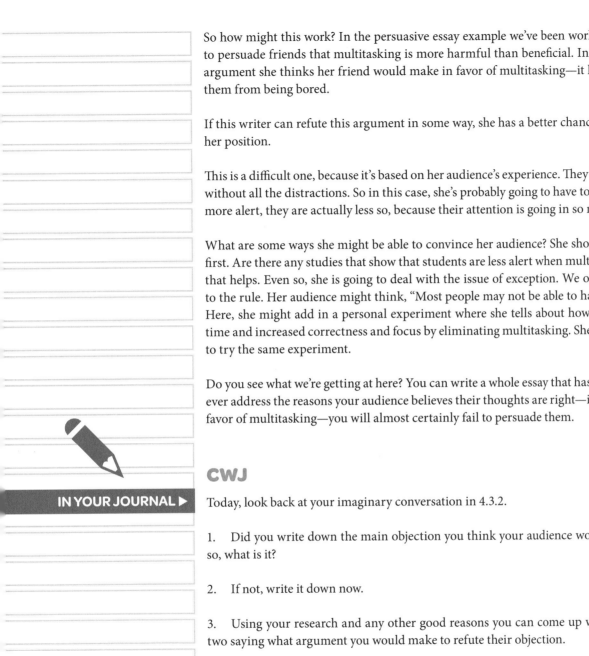

IN YOUR JOURNAL ▶

Today, look back at your imaginary conversation in 4.3.2.

1. Did you write down the main objection you think your audience would have to your argument? If so, what is it?

2. If not, write it down now.

3. Using your research and any other good reasons you can come up with, write down a sentence or two saying what argument you would make to refute their objection.

TESTING ARGUMENTS

Both when reading others' arguments and crafting your own, beware of **fallacious** statements and arguments. Logical fallacies **pervade** our world. We hear them so often that we often fail to recognize that the thinking behind them is faulty.

One of our favorites is the old cough syrup commercial where an actor recommended the product with this line: "I'm not a doctor, but I play one on TV." This is an appeal to authority. Sometimes appealing to an authority can bolster your argument. If the authority invented a new medicine that cured the flu, his expertise would be relevant. In this case, though, the "authority" isn't even a real doctor. How is any opinion he has on the effectiveness of cough syrup pertinent?

You can find lists of logical fallacies that are pages long on the Internet. We won't begin to try to cover all of them here, but here are a few to get you thinking. They may seem obvious. However, if we don't read carefully, a stylistically skilled writer can make some of these fallacies seem pretty appealing!

▶   "Post hoc, ergo propter hoc" is Latin for "after this, therefore because of this." It's assuming that because one event happens after another, the first caused the second.

Example: We know a man who once got a flu shot. Then he got the flu. He assumed that the shot caused him to get the flu. More likely, he got it because he was already getting sick when he got the shot, or the shot just didn't work. We've probably all committed this logical fallacy—but we need to make sure we don't do it (or fall for it!) in writing.

▶   Slippery Slope— This faulty reasoning implies that if you take a certain step in a particular direction, you will surely find yourself at the bottom of the slope.

Example: If you've ever seen the musical "*The Music Man,*" in the song "Ya Got Trouble," music man Harold sells musical instruments through slippery slope thinking. He paints a picture of how the town's children are going to go bad, beginning with a sip of wine for a cough. Just a few lines later, he predicts these same children will be gambling on horses and making a living shooting pool if they don't buy his instruments!

▶   Hasty Generalization—This fallacy occurs when you draw a conclusion with too few facts.

Example: "When I went to London, I got my backpack stolen. The British are thieves!" Having too few participants in a study or using a personal example as proof are similar errors in reasoning. The basic truth here is, "don't rush to judgment."

▶ Either/or—We discussed this at length in Unit 3. It's rare for an argument to only have two positions. Generally, when you reduce an argument this way, you're oversimplifying it.

Example: "If you don't vote for the new law raising the driving age to 18, you're voting in favor of more car accidents!" In this case, perhaps you are voting in favor of kids getting more driving experience with their parents before they go to college. Or for kids who need to work to be able to get to their jobs.

▶ Straw man—this is an oversimplification of an opponent's argument that you set up—like a straw man instead of a real one—so that you can easily knock it down.

Example: "Dr. Smith says video games make kids violent. He clearly hasn't researched the valuable critical thinking they learn from video games." In this case, he's oversimplifying the research. Dr. Smith isn't saying all video games make kids violent—he's studied those rated for mature audiences. And he's talking about kids who play at least 15 hours a week. Rather than looking at the opponent's real argument, this argument sets up a false one that is easier to knock down.

▶ Ad hominem—means "to the man." It's attacking the person rather than their argument.

Example: "You can't believe anything Professor Burns says because he's clearly a communist!" Even though you may not like the professor's politics and you would want to carefully test what he says. His arguments are what you should focus upon.

IN YOUR JOURNAL ▶

CWJ

Over the next 24 hours, keep your eyes and ears open for these logical fallacies. If you find a real-life example, record it in your journal in a short paragraph. If not, make up your own example based on one of these fallacies and write it in your journal.

STYLE TIME: USE COMMAS WHEN ADDING WORDS

 Simple subject-verb sentences don't need commas:
Dogs bite.
Cats scratch.
Tigers chase.

But when you start adding words to a simple subject-verb sentence—whether at the beginning, middle, or end—you often need a comma.

If you add words at the **beginning**, you often need a comma.
Dependent clause:
Although they make good pets, cats scratch when they feel trapped.

Introductory word:
However, dogs make better pets.

Introductory clause:
When I was gone, the package came.

If you add words at the **end** of a sentence, sometimes you need a comma.
To show contrast:
He is blind, not deaf.

SOMETIMES with a dependent clause if the sentence would be confusing without it.
Cats scratch when they feel trapped, although they make good pets.

Caution: With MOST dependent clauses, you need a comma at the beginning of a sentence, but not at the end. Compare:

Because she was late to class, she failed the quiz.
She failed the quiz because she was late to class.

You need a comma in the **middle** of a sentence IF the sentence conveys the same basic meaning without the comma.

So here you would need commas:
My mother, <u>who often travels</u>, is going to Germany.

And here you would not:
Cars <u>with bigger engines</u> require more fuel.

See how the second sentence wouldn't make any sense if you took the underlined words out? That's a good test to see if you need commas around phrases in the middle of a sentence.

THE RIGHT WORD

 Below are the five vocabulary words in context for this week. You should already have defined them in your journal as you found them in the reading.

1. Often the **missives** we send are short and to the point, with a clear message.
2. **Rhetoric** is the art of speaking or writing effectively.
3. In an argument, the section where you **refute** another argument is called rebuttal.
4. Both when reading others' arguments and crafting your own, beware of **fallacious** statements and arguments.
5. Logical fallacies **pervade** our world.

Using your thesaurus, try to find the BEST word to replace the bold word in the sentence. If you aren't familiar with the meanings of all the synonyms for each word in the thesaurus, you may need to use your dictionary to look them up. That way you can choose the word that best fits the sentence.

Write with WORLD

WHAT WRITERS WILL NEED FOR THIS LESSON:

▶ Your writer's journal
▶ Dictionary
▶ Thesaurus
▶ Post-it flags

WORLD WISDOM

We want you to go into this lesson feeling ready to write. Take a few moments to flip back through your CWJ. You've written a lot already. If you look at your writing at the beginning and compare it to what you can do now, we bet you'll notice significant progress.

You've learned some things about yourself as a writer—where you like to work, whether you like to write early in the morning or late at night, whether you need silence or noise in the background.

Some of you may not be sure what works best for you. That's okay. It takes time to develop your own particular writing process. Everyone's way of doing things is a little different. Today, we'll look at what three *God's World News* writers have to say about how the writing process works for them.

Writing an essay can be fun. Or it can drive you crazy.

When I write an essay, I try to follow some basic steps so that my writing is clear and interesting. Here's what I do.

First, I brainstorm. Once I decide what I am going to write about, say, how I feel about professional baseball, I just start jotting down any ideas that come to mind. I don't worry about punctuation or proper sentences. I write quickly, and by the time I finish, I have a messy page covered in scribbles, scratches, and questions.

Then, I divide it into logical chunks. If something doesn't fit, I scratch it out. If you're asked to write a five paragraph essay, then you probably need to divide your brainstorming into three parts. This allows for an opening paragraph, three body paragraphs and a conclusion.

Next, I narrow the topic; for example, I may focus on the use of steroids in professional baseball. This allows me to write with strong feelings and to be more specific. Broad topics are boring. Narrowed topics hold readers! After this, the rest is easy.

Then, I double-check my facts by doing some research. I may think steroids are still a real problem in pro baseball, but things change!

Now I grab the reader in my opening sentence. Something like: "Baseball players are the biggest drug users

in professional sports" will certainly get the reader's attention. An opening sentence like this shows how you feel and will cause the reader to keep going to see if you can defend what you just claimed.

After that, I use specific examples, cite names, and mention years and teams and facts. Again, be specific.

Now I'm ready to edit my essay. I recheck for spelling, punctuation, and grammar errors. Every rough draft has them. Does it all make sense? Is there a sentence that seems choppy or just odd?

Finally, I ask someone else to read it. Many times, we just cannot "hear" how our writing sounds to others. It's very important to have an editor. My wife is my editor and reads everything I write before I send it off for publication.

—Roy McGinnis

When I have a choice of topics for a general essay, I pick one I know the most about. Or else I choose one that interests me. I like to spend a few days just thinking about my topic. I jot down thoughts as they come. Once I begin writing, my scribbled notes will become paragraphs. I find other information to insert to support my views.

I work until I have a first draft that's longer than my final essay should be. Then I print it out and find a comfortable spot to edit—away from the computer. It's easier for me to re-organize my writing using pen and paper.

Striking out unnecessary words and lines takes the essay down to its essential theme. I replace other words to create clearer, stronger sentences.

Fresh eyes will catch most problems. I find someone to read my final draft. Or, I wait awhile before reading it again myself. Then I fix any trouble spots, and . . . finished!

—Patti Richter

When I write for God's World News, I'm telling other people's stories. In order to do that, I first have to learn their stories. I read articles online and check out books from the library. I work better when I put a space of at least one day between my research and my writing. Because I'm a process thinker, my brain needs time to sort through everything I just read. When I follow this self-prescribed protocol, my writing usually comes pretty easily.

I do most of my writing when my house is quiet and I'm alone. Since there are six of us who live here, that almost always means I write at night. Doing this allows me to then "sleep" on what I wrote, read through it the next morning, make necessary revisions, and then submit it for final review.

No matter how long I continue to do this or how much I enjoy doing it, I always feel relieved when a project has reached completion. It always feels really good.

—Megan Dunham

IN YOUR JOURNAL ▶

Did you notice that though the writers had some things in common, they all work somewhat differently? As you write, pay attention to your process. Figuring out how you work best will help you to become a more comfortable and efficient writer.

CAPSULE 1 4.4.1

INTRODUCING YOUR ESSAY

Whether you realize it or not, in the last three lessons, you've gathered the material and done much of the thinking necessary to write your persuasive essay. In this lesson, you will put it all together into a compelling argument geared toward convincing your readers.

In most cases, a single essay doesn't change a reader's mind on a topic. So, though it would show amazing rhetorical skill (and probably some natural talent) if you wrote an essay so dazzling that it converted readers to your opinion, it's unlikely that it will happen. You put forth your best arguments. If you can get your readers to consider your opinion, you've done your job. This partly explains why the professor in the 4.3.2 Professor's Office believes that the writer was successful: Amy put forward arguments strong enough to make her friend Emma consider her opinion—even when Emma disagreed with her.

Today, we want you to decide how to draw your readers in. How can you get them interested so that they will want to keep reading? Your first sentences need to grab their attention.

Often, students want to ease into an essay by generalizing about their topic: "Teens today are texting more than ever." This doesn't really tell your readers anything they don't already know. Would it get your attention? As teachers, when we see an essay that begins this way, we brace ourselves for an essay that is going to take some work to read. We pour another cup of coffee. If an essay starts off with a generalization, it usually doesn't get much more specific or interesting as it continues.

So how should you start? First, consider your audience. A startling statistic might grab adults, but would probably be less interesting to kids your age. On the other hand, a lyric to a popular song that's relevant might grab a younger audience, but would probably leave most adults scratching their heads. A personal anecdote or an analogy would probably work with both groups. (An analogy is a comparison of two things, usually using something simpler and more familiar to explain something more complex and difficult.) These are probably the best ways to grab attention, though if you have a really interesting fact or a compelling question, these can work too. (Just make sure you don't begin with a boring fact or question—these are too similar to boring generalizations.)

Once you have an idea of how you'll begin, move on to your CWJ for today.

IN YOUR JOURNAL ▶

Beginning with a great strategy is just part of what you need to accomplish in your introduction. Even more important, you must introduce the thesis or central argument of your essay. We won't prescribe how long your introduction should be, but in most cases it should take you one to three paragraphs to introduce and get to the main point of your essay. Here's an example to help give you a picture of what a good introduction looks like.

> I flipped through the article my mom had printed out and put on my desk. "Multitasking Teens May Be Muddling Their Brains," blared the headline. I scoffed. I knew multitasking wasn't hurting me. I got good grades. Multitasking kept me alert and engaged while I was doing homework. I had friends to help me when I got stuck on hard questions. Multitasking made me a better student. Besides, it was fun!
>
> But as I looked through the article, I began to worry a bit. I did some more research and a personal experiment. My conclusion? Multitasking can make teens feel more alert and engaged in their homework, but it actually slows them down. I believe that constant multitasking is more harmful than beneficial. It also decreases the ability to focus. Some studies suggest that multitasking could be preventing young brains from developing important connections.

Let's break this down into parts so that you can see each part of the thesis statement and where you will restate it and support it in the paper:

Statement of opinion: I believe that constant multitasking is more harmful than beneficial. (**This doesn't need to be restated in any specific place—this is simply the opinion you will use your points to prove. You can put it in your thesis statement wherever you think it best fits.**)

Rebuttal: Multitasking can make teens feel more alert and engaged in their homework, but it actually slows them down. (**Restate at the beginning of your paragraph or paragraphs that include the evidence supporting your rebuttal.**)

Reason 1: It also decreases the ability to focus. (**Restate at the beginning of your paragraph or paragraphs that include the evidence supporting this reason.**)

Reason 2: Some studies suggest that multitasking could be preventing young brains from developing important connections. (**Restate at the beginning of your paragraph or paragraphs that include the evidence supporting this reason.**)

Now it's your turn!

Even though this is a persuasive essay, you want to make sure you are present in it. In some way, you should include yourself. You should have stated your opinion in the first person (like the statement of opinion above). Throughout, include some other information that shows how the topic relates to your life. You want your readers to have some idea of why this topic is important to you.

Sometimes, teachers want you to limit yourself to presenting the facts, building a reasoned argument to persuade your audience in an academic paper. What we want you to do here is a little less formal—more like an opinion essay in the newspaper. We want to know who you are and what your stakes are in the argument. We think that makes the argument much more interesting.

We recommend drafting on the computer so that you can make revisions easily. If you don't draft on the computer, it's a good idea to leave some space so that you can make changes without having to squeeze things in so tightly that your changes are hard to read. If you're working on the computer, it's fine to wait until you have a finished draft to put in your CWJ. But don't forget! And always make sure to print out a copy or email yourself a copy so that if your computer crashes, your work isn't lost.

CAPSULE 2
4.4.2

REBUTTAL: ADDRESSING AUDIENCE ARGUMENTS

Regardless of where you decide to put it in your paper, we want you to write your rebuttal next. Often, it's a good idea to put your rebuttal argument first. That way you disarm your readers of what is probably their main argument before providing evidence supporting your position.

Just like the other parts of your argument, your rebuttal point should be forecasted in your thesis statement. If you haven't already added it, make sure to add your rebuttal to your thesis statement.

CWJ

Today, as you write your rebuttal section, make sure you:

1) Say what argument you are rebutting.
2) Develop your refutation using some combination of reasoning, proof, examples, and other evidence that bolsters your argument and disproves or casts doubt on the position your audience holds.
There is no set length for this section. It should be at least one well-developed paragraph, but it might be longer if you have more than one point or reason.

Here's our example of a rebuttal section.

◄ IN YOUR JOURNAL

Many students seem to feel the same way that I did—that multitasking doesn't hurt their ability to get work done. In fact, some even feel that they get more done. When I put out a status update on Facebook asking people to respond to the question, "How does multitasking affect your ability to work?" most thought it didn't hurt. Some thought it made them work better. "I think I actually get more done when I do several things at once," said one friend. "I used to get stuck on math problems and just give up," said another. "Now I text my friends and they help me figure out what I'm doing wrong."

I believe there's some truth to my friends' points. Multitasking some of the time—especially on an easy subject or when you need help—can be beneficial. Experts like Dr. Jay Giedd, a neuroscientist for the National Institute of Health, think multitasking can be a good thing for teens. He says, "They'll get good at multitasking, which they'll likely be doing at their adult jobs" (Carroll).

Multitasking with lots of electronic devices is so new that experts agree that we can't know for sure if there will be any long-term impacts. However, studies on multitasking are not new. The evidence clearly points to the fact that no matter how a teen may feel when multitasking, they are not more productive. David E. Meyer is director of the Brain, Cognition, and Action Laboratory at the University of Michigan. He's done lots of studies on the brain. He says that when people try to do two or more things at the same time, they make lots more mistakes than they would if they did one thing at a time. It also takes a lot longer—double the time or even more (Wallis). That makes sense. Plenty of other studies I read about show that people's brains can't really do two things at once—you're really switching back and forth. Often, you have to start your thinking all over again each time you switch tasks. Multitasking can be a huge time waster. So, though multitasking may make people feel more efficient, the evidence clearly demonstrates that our brains cannot do two things at once, and when we try, we may actually hurt our productivity.

CAPSULE 3 4.4.3

PRESENTING YOUR REASONS

Once you've refuted what you believe is your audience's main reason for opposing your argument, you're ready to move on to your other reasons. Look back at your thesis statement from the section you wrote in 4.4.1. In what order have you organized your reasons? Since your thesis statement serves as a map for the essay, you'll want to make sure you follow the order you laid out in your thesis.

However, now that you've gathered all your research and thought through your arguments, you may want to change the order of your reasons. That's because you want to put them in the most effective order possible. Do any of the ideas build on each other? Sometimes an argument works that way. You have to prove one thing in order to prove the next. For instance, if you are trying to show that young adults staying dependent on their parents longer is caused by overprotective parents, you would first have to show that young adults ARE dependent on their parents longer. Then you would need to rule out other reasons (like a bad economy and rising college costs). Do you see how order is important here?

Otherwise, it's good to start with a strong point. If you have a weaker point, put it in the middle. Save your best point for last. (That's if you have three points. If you have fewer, end with your best reason.)

CWJ

Here is the "reasons" section of the model essay. Notice how the author uses the research of experts to prove her point, but also adds in her own reasoning at times. Also, note that she begins paragraphs 1 and 2 with topic sentences that restate "reason 1" and "reason 2" from her thesis statement. By referring back to her thesis statement "map," she helps lead her readers through her argument so that they always know where she is going and they don't get lost in the argument.

◀ IN YOUR JOURNAL

Another good reason to limit multitasking is that it decreases a person's ability to focus. A study published in the Proceedings of the National Academy of Sciences in 2006 led by neuroscience professor Russell Poldrack tested the impact of multitasking on people's ability to focus. They sorted cards. Sometimes, they listened to a series of beeps and had to keep track of the number of high-pitched ones mentally. Other times, they just sorted. The results showed that when they were multitasking, they couldn't really focus on the cards. When only doing one task at a time, participants learned more. When they multitasked, they couldn't answer certain questions about the cards. They were actually using different kinds of memory when multitasking and focusing. The focused memory allows you to develop a deeper understanding (Clay). If you're multitasking all the time, you lose out on this deeper type of learning that you do when you are focused. You may not be able to remember information long term. Your ability to apply knowledge—not just remember facts—may be compromised too (Golovan).

Perhaps the most compelling reason to limit multitasking is that, as a young person, your brain is still developing—up until you're 25 or even 30 years old. While your brain has 93 percent of its size by the time you are six, Dr. Giedd says lots of work is still going on inside the structure: "Different parts of the brain are being connected up." While he isn't particularly worried about the consequences, some doctors are beginning to see patients with problems. In an interview, Dr. Beth Hellerstein, a professor at Case Western Reserve School of Medicine, says she's beginning to see patients who have developed symptoms of Attention Deficit Disorder (ADD) from too much multitasking. "Teens heading off to college are finding it's difficult to stay focused," she says. "Sitting in a quiet room and tuning out the distractions is challenging" (Golovan). Since the 1980s, research has shown a link between media use and ADD.

I did a little more research. According to a study by Northwestern University, ADHD cases in kids younger than 18 increased 66 percent from 2000 to 2010 (Lee). Though it's impossible to say for sure that too much media is the cause, this statistic raises the question—especially since media usage has gone up exponentially in the same period. In 2004, kids were consuming over 6 hours a day of media—but they were packing in 8 hours of content. In 2010, they were up to seven and a half hours. With multitasking, that's a whopping 11 hours a day of content!

Today as you write, make sure:
1. You don't just mash together a bunch of source material. When you quote something, you need to then explain why you quoted it for your readers. You need to provide the logical links showing how all the information fits together. Each time you quote or paraphrase a writer, ask yourself, "How does it fit into my argument?" Then include any necessary explanation.
2. Cite your source so you don't forget where the material came from. Put the author's last name in parenthesis after a quote or paraphrase.

CAPSULE 4 4.4.4

SUMMING UP AND MAKING A FINAL PLEA

You're almost there! Today, you need to finish strong. A conclusion should only take a paragraph or two at most. You want to reiterate your points, summing them up in as persuasive a manner as possible. You might add a final example if you think it could help sway your audience. End with a statement that leaves your reader thinking, if possible.

That's it. When you're ready, move on to your CWJ and read the sample conclusion.

CWJ

While the phenomenon of media multitasking is too new to say for sure whether it causes problems for developing brains, it's probably best to practice focusing sometimes too. We know multitasking makes us less productive. Whether we feel it's true or not, the research is clear. Multitasking makes focusing more difficult. And without focusing on one thing at a time, we may not be learning it in the same in-depth way. Who wants to risk wiring your brain the wrong way, possibly creating ADD symptoms? It seems like moderation in multitasking is the best way to go.

All of this evidence is pretty convincing. Even so, it was a little hard for me to believe. So I did my own experiment. For one week, I kept track of how many problems I missed in math and how long it took me to do my math homework each night while multitasking. The next week, I did my math at the kitchen table with no devices around me (except for my calculator). The time seemed to go more slowly. It was boring. But I have to admit, the statistics from my own personal study matched those of professionals. It took me less time—and I did a little better too. Though I'm sure I won't give up multitasking altogether, researching this topic made me realize the need for learning to focus too.

When you've finished reading, write your conclusion.

CITING YOUR SOURCES

To complete your paper, you'll need to make a list of the sources you've used. Various handbooks will give you different instructions on how to do this. However, the purposes of a works cited page are 1) to give the people whose ideas you are using credit for those ideas, and 2) to give your readers enough information to find those sources again should they want to research the topic further.

Here's a checklist to help you create a works cited page that meets these requirements:
1. Center "Works Cited" at the top of the page.
2. Put the sources in alphabetical order by author's last name.
3. Include the following information for each citation:

Last name, First name. "Title of Article." *Title of Magazine or Website*. Date of the
article. Web. Date you accessed the material.

Works Cited

Carroll, Linda. "Will Teen Multitasking Give Rise to ADD? Study May Offer Answer." *MSNBC*. 12 April 2011. Web. 6 June 2012.

Clay, Rebecca. "Mini-multitaskers." *American Psychological Association* 40.2. February 2009. Web. 6 June 2012.

Golovan, Lisa. "Is Multitasking Helpful or Harmful to Teenagers?" *Your Teen For Parents*. January 2011. Web. 6 June 2012.

Hamilton, John. "Multitasking Teens May Be Muddling Their Brains." *NPR*. 9 October 2008. Web. 6 June 2012.

Lee, Oliver. "Adderall: Crack or Cure-All?" *Take Part*. 6 April 2012. Web. 7 June 2012.

Wallis, Claudia. "genM: The Multitasking Generation." *Time Magazine*. 27 March 2006. Web. 6 June 2012.

MAKING CHANGES

Congratulations! You've written a persuasive essay. We can attest that many incoming college freshmen don't know how to do that. If you've grasped the essentials of the persuasive argument, you are light years ahead of many of your peers.

Even more important to you as a Christian, you've developed the ability to think critically. We hope what you've learned in *Write with WORLD II* has made you a better writer. Even more importantly, we hope it has taught you to seek truth and to "take every thought captive to obey Christ" (2 Corinthians 10:5).

As you seek truth, it's essential that you are in conversation with others. As Proverbs 27:17 says, "Iron sharpens iron, and one man sharpens another." What we want you to do today is ask a member of the audience that you chose (Parents? Friends?) to read through your essay. Choose someone whom you trust—someone whose opinion you respect and who will give you honest feedback. Have that person answer the following questions about your essay:

1. What is the writer's topic? What is her opinion on that topic?
2. Did the writer guess your main argument against her position?
3. If NOT, what is your main argument against her position?
4. What was her most convincing reason? Why?
5. Were there any reasons she gave that were not convincing? What would make this point stronger? (More evidence? An example? More explanation?)
6. What did you like best about this paper?
7. What is one thing you might change?
8. Does the essay have a title? If not, suggest one.

Once you've had a chance to look over your audience member's answers, make the changes they suggest. (If you don't agree with the changes they suggest, discuss them with a parent or teacher so that they can help you decide if they are needed.)

Also, have you given your essay a title? If not, do so now. Like your introduction, try to think of something that will grab your reader's interest so that he will want to know more.

CWJ

Today, after making any changes your audience reader thought you needed, give a copy of your paper to your teacher. Ask your teacher to mark the following things using colored pencils:

RED—underline a favorite sentence in the essay. This might be a great example, a really well-worded sentence, a great image, or an instance where you reason particularly well.

ORANGE—underline good word choices—strong verbs, interesting adjectives, "right words" or other great vocabulary.

PURPLE—underline spots that could be improved with more explanation and/or the student making more logical links between ideas.

BLUE—underline sentences that you find confusing or hard to understand. In the margin, please write some questions or comments to help the student see what is missing or what caused confusion.

PINK—circle any misused commas.

At the end, write a note telling the writer what you liked about her persuasive essay.

Once your reader returns the essay, revise your essay, making the final changes.

STYLE TIME

i Take one last look over your essay for grammar issues. Pay special attention to commas. Remember the three basic rules for when you need commas:

1. To avoid confusion
   ▶ Separate items in a series: *John, Granger, Mary, Margaret, and Bobby*
   ▶ When directly addressing someone: *Fred, read your book.*
   ▶ To prevent misunderstandings: *Children who can, swim three laps.*

2. To separate independent clauses: *He took the train to Rome, and then he flew to London.*

3. When adding words to the beginning, middle, or end of a sentence.
   ▶ When adding an introductory word, introductory clause, or dependent clause:
     When I am sick, I like to drink Sprite.
   ▶ When adding words that are not necessary (nonrestrictive clauses and phrases) to a sentence:
     My mother, who often travels, is going to Germany.

Reminder: if the meaning of the sentence is changed without the words, you DON'T need commas. (This type of clause or phrase is restrictive. That means it's necessary to the sentence.)

▶ SOMETIMES when adding words to the end of a sentence: to show contrast and with a dependent clause when it would be confusing without a comma: *Cats scratch when they feel trapped, although they make good pets.*

When you finish checking your grammar and your teacher agrees that your final draft is complete, you're finished. Nice work!

THE RIGHT WORD

Here are the 15 words we studied in this unit. Match each word in the first column with the synonym from the second column that BEST expresses its meaning:

_____ 1. profound	a. hostile
_____ 2. axiom	b. amass
_____ 3. conduit	c. deep
_____ 4. lexicon	d. message
_____ 5. inimical	e. dictionary
_____ 6. scrutiny	f. false
_____ 7. viable	g. channel
_____ 8. preponderance	h. inspection
_____ 9. resilient	i. workable
_____ 10. garnered	j. weight
_____ 11. missives	k. flexible
_____ 12. rhetoric	l. spread
_____ 13. refute	m. contradict
_____ 14. fallacious	n. eloquence
_____ 15. pervade	o. rule

In *Write with WORLD II* you've learned 60 new words. We hope you will try to work these into your speech and writing—and that you'll keep working to augment your vocabulary!